Righteous Giving to the Poor: *Tzedakah* ("Charity") in Classical Rabbinic Judaism

Gorgias Handbooks

Series Editor

George Anton Kiraz

Gorgias Handbooks provides students and scholars with reference books, textbooks and introductions to different topics or fields of study. In this series, Gorgias welcomes books that are able to communicate information, ideas and concepts effectively and concisely, with useful reference bibliographies for further study.

Righteous Giving to the Poor: *Tzedakah* ("Charity") in Classical Rabbinic Judaism

Including a Brief Introduction to Rabbinic Literature

By

Rivka Ulmer

Moshe Ulmer

gorgias press

2014

Gorgias Press LLC, 954 River Road, Piscataway, NJ, 08854, USA

www.gorgiaspress.com

2014

ISBN 978-1-4632-0261-3 ISSN 1935-6838

Library of Congress Cataloging-in-Publication Data

Ulmer, Rivka.
Righteous giving to the poor : tzedakah ("charity") in classical rabbinic Judaism : including a brief introduction to rabbinic literature / by Rivka Ulmer [and] Moshe Ulmer.
pages cm
Includes bibliographical references.
ISBN 978-1-4632-0261-3
1. Charity. 2. Charity laws and legislation (Jewish law) 3. Rabbinical literature--History and criticism. I. Ulmer, Moshe. II. Title.
BJ1286.C5U46 2014
296.3'677--dc23

2014010748

Printed in the United States of America

TABLE OF CONTENTS

Table of Contents v
Abbreviations vii
Transliteration ix
A Brief Introduction to Rabbinic Literature 1
  The Origins of Rabbinic Judaism 1
  Foundational Texts of Classical Rabbinic Judaism 3
    Mishnah 4
    Talmud 13
    Midrash 23
  Inner-Biblical Interpretation 24
  Introduction to *Tzedakah* ("Charity") in Judaism 39
Chapter One: Theology of *Tzedakah* 45
Chapter Two: The Rabbinic View of Poverty and the Humiliation of Accepting *Tzedakah* 57
Chapter Three: The Rewards of Giving *Tzedakah* 69
  Eligibility to Obtain the Reward 69
  The Power of *Tzedakah* 71
  Reciprocity of Benefit Between the Donor and the Donee ... 73
  Benefits Obtained During One's Lifetime 75
  The Miracle Stories 77
  Benefits in the World to Come 83

Chapter Four: The Penalty of Not Giving *Tzedakah*....89
Chapter Five: The Role of *Tzedakah* in the Community....93
Chapter Six: The Urgency of Giving *Tzedakah*....99
Chapter Seven: Giving *Tzedakah* Discreetly and Indirectly....103
Chapter Eight: Rules Affecting the Donor of *Tzedakah*....109
Chapter Nine: Alms Collectors....115
Chapter Ten: The Priorities in Giving *Tzedakah*....121
Chapter Eleven: Vows and *Tzedakah*....129
Chapter Twelve: Motivation in Giving *Tzedakah*....137
Chapter Thirteen: *Tzedakah* in Relation to other *Mitzvot*....141
Chapter Fourteen: *Tzedakah* in Respect to Shabbat and Fast Days....147
Chapter Fifteen: Biblical Figures Performing *Tzedakah*....151
Chapter Sixteen: Restrictions upon the Donee and Receiving *Tzedakah* Fraudulently....157
Chapter Seventeen: *Tzedakah* and the Gentile Community....163
Conclusion....167
Rabbinic Authorities....169
Glossary....173
Bibliography....177
Rabbinic Literature....177
Secondary Literature....182

ABBREVIATIONS

b.	ben, bar (son of)
BCE	Before the Common Era
CE	Common Era
R.	Rabbi, Rav

TRANSLITERATION

א -
ב b,v
ג g
ד d
ה h
ו v
ז z
ח *ḥ*
ט t
י y
כ k, kh
ל l
מ m
נ n
ס s
ע ʻ
פ p, f
צ tz
ק k
ר r
ש s,sh
ת t

In addition, it should be noted that doubling of consonants was rarely utilized except for words that have become part of the English language, such as Rabbi and *Gittin*.

A Brief Introduction to Rabbinic Literature

The Origins of Rabbinic Judaism

The origins of rabbinic Judaism are found in the many Judaisms that co-existed during the Second Temple period in the Land of Israel, when biblical and co-biblical texts (Pseudepigrapha, Apocrypha, Dead Sea Scrolls, and others) were edited and interpreted. Classical rabbinic Judaism flourished from the first century CE to the closure of the *Babylonian Talmud*, c. 600 CE, in Babylonia. Among the different groups of Jews in antiquity, rabbinic Judaism held that at Mount Sinai God revealed the Torah to Moses in two media, the Written and the Oral Torah. The Rabbis claimed they possessed the memorized or Oral Torah. Classical rabbinic Judaism is separated into different strata, e.g., Tannaitic (until 200 CE), Amoraic (200–500 CE), Saboraic (500 CE – seventh century). The first stage of formative rabbinic Judaism is represented by the *Mishnah*, a law code that came to closure c. 200 CE, after the destruction of the Second Temple of Jerusalem in 70 CE by the Romans and the defeat of the Bar Kokhba War in 132–135 CE. Rabbinic Judaism interpreted the Torah, often in opposition to the priestly tradition, which was committed to the written tradition and the sacrificial cult of the Temple. However, at the end of its formative period rabbinic Judaism synthesized the interpretive, messianic and priestly traditions. Rabbinic Judaism produced many different texts, ranging from the *Mishnah* and *Tosefta* to *Midrashic* texts and the two Talmuds. Rabbinic Judaism continued to flourish in the Middle Ages in the Diaspora. Today it represents "normative" Judaism, the Jewish religious expression of a substantial portion of the world-wide Jewish community.

The sources of rabbinic Judaism are located in the Second Temple Period, during which the reconstructed Temple in Jerusalem existed between 516 BCE and 70 CE. Interpretations of the

Bible multiplied during this time leading to para-rabbinic and pre-rabbinic conceptions. The history of the formative period of Judaism entails the destruction of the Jerusalem Temple in 70 CE and the emergence of rabbinic Judaism under the Roman occupation of the Land of Israel until the Arab conquest in the seventh century; the entire period is described and analyzed by Alon.[1] The extent of Jewish autonomy under the Roman Empire, the towns and cities, as well as uprisings and the Bar Kokhba War, are important in understanding the emergence and consolidation of the rabbinic movement. Furthermore, the development and spread of rabbinic thought in the Diaspora, the relations between the national center in the Land of Israel (Roman Palestine) and the communities abroad are also analyzed by Alon. Under Roman occupation the Land of Israel suffered agricultural decline and the majority of farmers consisted of tenants on the estates of powerful overlords; the extent of this decline is analyzed by Sperber.[2] Schwartz focuses upon Roman imperialism and its influence upon the Land, [3] as well as its inhabitants in a broad study that in some areas supplements

---

[1] Gedaliah Alon, *The Jews in their Land in the Talmudic Age*. Cambridge, Mass.: Harvard University Press, 1989. Presents a coherent narrative of the Land of Israel, beginning with the destruction of Jerusalem and the Jewish Commonwealth by the Romans until the Arab conquest. Analyses of life under Roman rule, economic conditions and social welfare, the legal system, resistance movements, controversies, and the emergence of the Sages as community leaders after 70 CE make this book indispensable.

[2] Daniel Sperber, *Roman Palestine: 200–400. The Land* (Ramat-Gan: Bar Ilan University Press, 1978) addresses the radical change that took place in the agrarian community during the third and fourth centuries CE and presents analyses of crop-yields, transfer of property from Jews to non-Jews. Discusses mills and viniculture, as well as famine, droughts and plagues. Provides explanations of common Greek terms, such as *epitropoi* (procurators).

[3] Seth Schwartz, *Imperialism and Jewish Society 200 BCE to 640 CE* (Princeton, NJ: Princeton University Press, 2001). A historical analysis of the influence of Roman imperialism on the political, economic and religious development of Jewish life and rabbinic Judaism in the Land of Israel.

Alon and Sperber. Schäfer offers a very condensed history of the Second Temple and rabbinic period,[4] whereas Cohen is a more theologically based compact historical survey.[5]

FOUNDATIONAL TEXTS OF CLASSICAL RABBINIC JUDAISM

This book is based to a great extent upon the foundational texts of classical rabbinic Judaism.[6] Several texts of rabbinic Judaism are so

---

[4] Peter Schäfer, *The History of the Jews in the Greco-Roman World* (London: Routledge, 2003).This textbook offers a concise introductory political history, beginning with Alexander the Great, continuing with Ptolemaic Rule, Seleucid Rule, Hasmoneans, Herod the Great, the Jewish Wars, Bar Kokhba Revolt and ending with the Arab conquest. This survey acknowledges that the source material is often inconsistent for the period summarized.

[5] Shaye Cohen, *From the Maccabees to the Mishnah* (Louisville, KY: Westminster John Knox, 2006). Explores the sects of Judaism from 170 BCE – 200 CE, beginning with the Maccabean revolt, and working through the Pharisees, the Sadducees, the Essenes, the nascent Christian movement, and Jewish people in the Mediterranean world. Cohen argues that Judaism was always a religion that emphasized practice and tradition over doctrine.

[6] Günter Stemberger, *Introduction to the Talmud and Midrash* (Edinburgh: T& T Clark, 2nd edition, 1996). The book is divided into three sections: general introduction, Talmudic literature, and *Midrashim*. The novice will find hermeneutic rules, abbreviated historical facts and lists of Rabbis. The book contains a meticulous bibliography, including references to books, articles and text editions, as well as Hebrew manuscripts. Jacob Neusner, *Introduction to Rabbinic Literature* (New York: Doubleday, 1994), presents an extensive introduction to rabbinic literature. A general introduction is followed by a presentation of different rabbinic texts, referred to as "documents." He introduces the Judaism represented by rabbinic Judaism and defines rabbinic literature and its principal parts. Texts presented include the *Mishnah*, *Tosefta*, the two Talmuds, as well as the different types of *Midrash*. Shmuel Safrai, Zeev Safrai, Joshua Schwartz, and Peter J. Tomson, *The Literature of the Sages. First Part* (Minneapolis: Fortress, 2007; *Second Part.* Assen: Van Gorcum, 2006). A monumental work containing descriptions of all major rabbinic works and the methodologies

important that they are referred to in virtually any discussion of Jewish concepts until today. Set forth below are brief introductions to the *Mishnah* and *Tosefta*, the *Jerusalem* and *Babylonian Talmud* and (rabbinic) *Midrash*.

Mishnah

The *Mishnah* is the first major written redaction of the Jewish oral traditions called the "Oral Torah."[7] It designates the collection of

---

applied to them. Informs the reader about the contents of each work, as well as its genre and its role within the canon. The book presents established methods of reading and researching rabbinic texts. Ephraim E. Urbach, *The Sages: Their Concepts and Beliefs* (Cambridge: Harvard University Press, 1987). A ground-breaking work that systematically interpreted rabbinic literature by focusing upon its major concepts, such as the belief in One God, the Presence of God in the World (*shekhinah*), the Celestial Retinue, the acceptance of the "Yoke of the Kingdom of Heaven." Solomon Schechter, *Aspects of Rabbinic Theology... introduction by Neil Gillman* (Woodstock, Vt.: Jewish Lights, 1999; repr. of the first edition, Philadelphia: The Jewish Publication Society, 1909). The book assembles the major concepts of rabbinic thought and offers a synthesis of rabbinic teachings based upon multiple sources. Barry W. Holtz, *Back to the Sources: Reading the Classic Jewish Texts* (Philadelphia: The Jewish Publication Society, 1984). This collection contains essays that introduce the *Talmud*, *Midrash*, Bible commentaries and prayer. This book is useful for the initial understanding of the different expressions of rabbinic literature and other genres, such as Jewish philosophy, that were influenced by rabbinic thought. John Bowker, *The Targums and Rabbinic Literature: An Introduction to Jewish Interpretations of Scripture* (Cambridge: Cambridge University Press, 2009). The Aramaic Targums consist of interpretive translations of the Hebrew Bible, which originated in synagogue teaching, where an interpretation of the biblical text had to be given orally for the benefit of non-Hebrew speaking congregations. The Targums share many interpretations with rabbinic literature.

[7] Hanokh Albek, *Shishah Sidre Mishnah* (Hebrew) (Jerusalem: Mosad Bialik, 1952), is the standard edition of the *Mishnah* in Hebrew with comments by the editor. Herbert Danby, *The Mishnah* (Oxford: Oxford University Press, 1933), is an older scholarly English translation that includes footnotes. Jacob Neusner, *The Mishnah: A New Translation* (New Haven:

rabbinic traditions redacted by Rabbi Yehudah Ha-Nasi (often referred to as "Rabbi") at the beginning of the third century CE.[8] The *Mishnah* reflects statements made between the first century BCE and second century CE by Sages. According to the *Iggeret* (Epistle) of Rav Sherira Gaon (c. 906–1006), after the tremendous upheaval caused by the destruction of the Temple and the Bar Kochba War (132–136 CE), the Oral Torah was in danger of being forgotten, and the *Mishnah* was written.

The *Mishnah* is the written authority secondary only to the *Tanakh* (Hebrew Bible) as a basis for the passing of judgment, a source and a tool for creating laws, and a work that complements the Bible. The contents of the *Mishnah* are the product of an ongoing process of elaborating and explaining the foundations, the details and the significance of the Torah's commandments. This process began long before the redaction of the *Mishnah*, and continued throughout the Talmudic period (first to sixth centuries CE) and beyond. Nevertheless, the *Mishnah* serves as the foundation for both the *Jerusalem Talmud* and the *Babylonian Talmud*. Through these works the *Mishnah* has shaped most of the actual practice of the Jewish religion down to the present day.

The redaction and dissemination of the *Mishnah* in the early third century marked a turning point in the history of rabbinic literature. Sages who were active up to the time of Rabbi Yehudah Ha-Nasi and his immediate disciples were called *Tannaim* (teachers of *Mishnah*).[9] The later *Amoraim* (Talmudic and Midrashic scholars) accepted the traditions of the *Tannaim* as authoritative. Tannaitic literature consists primarily of the *Mishnah*, the *Tosefta* (a collection similar to the *Mishnah*), and Tannaitic *Midrashim* (e.g., *Sifra*, *Sifré*, and *Mekhilta*).

Yale University Press, reprint 1991), an English translation that presents the text in an organized, readable manner.

[8] Jacob Neusner, *Making the Classics in Judaism* (Atlanta: Scholars Press, 1989), 1–13 and 19–44, pertains to the redaction of the text.

[9] Reuben Margaliot, *Yesod ha-Mishnah va-ʿarikhatah: seḳirah kelalit ʿal hishtalshelutah mi-yemot anshe keneset ha-gedolah ʿad ḥatimatah, ve-tokhnit sidurah* (Jerusalem: Mosad ha-Rav Kook, 1955) (Hebrew), important early scholarly investigation of Mishnaic composition and traditions.

Generally, the *Mishnah* complements, clarifies and systematizes the commandments of the Torah. For example, the Torah commands: *Remember the Sabbath day* (Exod. 20:8). The *Mishnah* provides this abstraction with a concrete practice, namely, the *kiddush* and *havdalah* rituals which mark the beginning and the ending of the Sabbath. The Torah also commands: *Observe the Sabbath day* (Deut. 5:12), and the *Mishnah* specifies thirty-nine major categories of prohibited labor, subsuming other kinds of labor under these thirty-nine categories. Furthermore, the Torah states: *When you eat and are satisfied, give thanks to your God for the good land which He has given you* (Deut. 8:10), while the *Mishnah* contains the wording of specific blessings to be recited before and after the consumption of different foods. It also extends the recitation of blessings to additional areas of human life, detailing blessings to be recited before and after the performance of commandments, blessings of praise and thanksgiving, and establishing a regular order of daily prayers, for example:

> "From what time on [may people] recite the evening *shemaʿ*?[10] From the hour that the priests come in to eat of their Heave-offering, until the end of the first watch; [these are] R. Eliʿezer's words, but the Sages say, Until midnight. R. Gamaliel says, Until the first light of dawn."[11]

The *Mishnah* organizes rules into a consistent system, for example concerning leprosy in Lev. 13–14. Several laws, the laws of *tzitzit* (ritual fringes), *tefillin* (phylacteries), *mezuzah* (the scroll inside a case with Deut. 6:4–9 mounted on a door post), the holiday of *Hanukkah*, and the laws of *gerim* (converts), are not elaborated upon in the *Mishnah*. These were later discussed in the so-called minor tractates of the *Babylonian Talmud*. Beyond halakhic issues the *Mishnah* teaches many ethical lessons:

> "Ben Zoma said: Who is wise? He who learns from all men, as it is written: *I have gained understanding from all my teachers* (Ps. 119:99).

---

[10] Deut. 6:4.

[11] *Mishnah*, Berakhot 1:1.

> Who is mighty? He who subdues his passions, as it is written: *One who is slow to anger is better than the mighty, and one whose temper is controlled than one who captures a city* (Prov. 16:32).
>
> Who is rich? He who rejoices in his portion, as it is written: *You shall eat the fruit of the labor of your hands; you shall be happy, and it shall go well with you* (Ps. 128:2). *You shall be* refers to this world; *and it shall be well with you* refers to the world to come.
>
> Who is honored? He that honors his fellow men as it is written: *For those who honor me I will honor, and those who despise me shall be treated with contempt* (1 Sam. 2:30)."[12]

The *Mishnah* teaches the oral traditions by presenting cases being brought to a resolution, usually along with the debate on the matter and the judgment that was given by a Rabbi based on the *halakhah*, *mitzvot*, and spirit of the teaching ("Torah") that guided his well-reasoned decision. The *Mishnah* does not claim to be the development of new laws, but rather the collection of existing traditions.

The *Mishnah* consists of six orders (*sedarim*), each *seder* (order) containing several tractates (*masekhtot*), sixty-three in total, and further subdivided into chapters and paragraphs or verses. The *Mishnah* is also called *Shas* (an acronym for *Shisha Sedarim* — the "six orders"). The *Talmud* scholar, Reʾuven Margolies (1889–1971) posited that there were originally seven orders of the *Mishnah*, referring to a Geonic tradition (after 600 CE) mentioning the existence of a seventh order containing the *stam* (statements without attribution) and *Berakhot* (blessings). In each order (with the exception of *Zeraʿim*), tractates are arranged from the largest (concerning the number of chapters) to the smallest.

The orders of the *Mishnah* and their subjects are:

I. *Zeraʿim* ("Seeds"), dealing with prayer and blessings, tithes and agricultural laws (eleven tractates). 1. *Berakhot*; 2. *Peʾah*; 3. *Demai*; 4. *Kilʾayim*; 5. *Sheviʿit*; 6. *Terumot*; 7. *Maʿaserot*; 8. *Maʿaser Sheni*; 9. *Ḥallah*; 10. *ʿOrlah*; 11. *Bikkurim*.

---

[12] *Pirke Avot* 4:1

II. *Moᶜed* ("Festival"), concerning the laws of the Sabbath and the Festivals (twelve tractates). 1. *Shabbat*; 2. *ᶜEruvin*; 3. *Pesaḥim*; 4. *Shekalim*; 5. *Yoma*; 6. *Sukkah*; 7. *Betzah*; 8. *Rosh Ha-Shanah*; 9. *Taᶜanit*; 10. *Megillah*; 11. *Moᶜed Katan*; 12. *Ḥagigah.*

III. *Nashim* ("Women"), concerning marriage and divorce, oaths and the laws of the nazirite (seven tractates). 1. *Yevamot*; 2. *Ketubbot*; 3. *Nedarim*; 4. *Nazir*; 5. *Sotah*; 6. *Gittin*; 7. *Kiddushin.*

IV. *Nezikin* ("Damages"), dealing with civil and criminal law, the functioning of the courts and oaths (ten tractates). 1. *Bava Kamma*; 2. *Bava Metziᶜa*; 3. *Bava Batra*; 4. *Sanhedrin*; 5. *Makkot*; 6. *Shevuᶜot*; 7. *ᶜEduyot*; 8. *ᶜAvodah Zarah*; 9. *Avot*; 10. *Horayot.*

V. *Kodashim* ("Holy things"), regarding sacrificial rites, the Temple, and the dietary laws (eleven tractates). 1. *Zevaḥim;* 2. *Menaḥot*; 3. *Ḥullin*; 4. *Bekhorot*; 5. *ᶜArakhin*; 6. *Temurah*; 7. *Keritot*; 8. *Meᶜilah*; 9. *Tamid*; 10. *Middot*; 11. *Kinnim.*

VI. *Toharot* ("Purities"), pertaining to the laws of purity and impurity, including the impurity of the dead, the laws of food purity and bodily purity (twelve tractates). 1. *Kelim*; 2. *Oholot*; 3. *Negaᶜim*; 4. *Parah*; 5. *Toharot*; 6. *Mikvaʾot*; 7. *Niddah*; 8. *Makhshirin*; 9. *Zavim*; 10. *Tevul Yom*; 11. *Yadayim*; 12. *ᶜUktzim.*

There is also a tradition that Ezra the Scribe (active c. 480–440 BCE) dictated from memory not only the twenty-four books of the *Tanakh* (Hebrew Bible) but sixty "extra-canonical" books. Traditionally, this was viewed as a reference to the *Mishnah* — rabbinic Judaism is often "ahistorical" — but it may be argued that the *Mishnah* does consist of sixty tractates, although the current number of tractates adds up to sixty-three. Tractate *Makkot* was originally part of tractate *Sanhedrin*, and tractates *Bava Kamma*, *Bava Metziᶜa* and *Bava Batra* may be regarded as subdivisions of a tractate *Nezikin.* According to another tradition, Hillel the Elder (110 BCE – c. 10 CE) organized the tractates into six orders to facilitate recitation. A mnemonic that is used to remember the sequence of the orders was provided by Rabbi Shimᶜon ben Lakish (*Babylonian Talmud,* Shabbat 31a); it is based on "And there shall be *faith* in your times, *strength*, *salvation*, *wisdom*, and *knowledge*" (Isa. 33:6). "Faith" refers to *Zera^cim* (Seeds), because a farmer sowing the crop must have faith to believe God will provide an abundant harvest. "Your times" refers to *Mo^ced* (Festival). "Strength" refers to order *Nashim* (Women). "Salvation" refers to *Nezikin* (Damages) because civil law "saves" people from each other. "Wisdom" refers to *Kodashim* (Holy Things) and "Knowledge" refers to *Taharot* (Purities) because they are difficult to understand. An acronym for the order of the *Mishnah* tractates is another mnemonic "*ZeMaN NaKaT*."

Rabbinic Judaism claims that the oral tradition was received by Moses at Mount Sinai at the same time as the *Five Books of Moses*, the Written Torah (*Torah she-bi-khtav*), and that these together have always been the basis of Jewish law (*halakhah*). Therefore, the Oral Law (*Torah she-be^cal-peh*) was also given to Moses at Sinai, and is the exposition of the Written Law as transmitted by the religious leaders of each generation. *Pirke Avot* ("the Ethics of the Fathers") of the *Mishnah* states:

> "Moses received the Torah from Sinai and transmitted it to Joshua; Joshua to the elders; the elders to the prophets; and the prophets handed it down to the men of the Great Assembly. They said three things: Be deliberate in judgment, raise up many disciples, and make a fence around the Torah. 2. Shim^con the Righteous was one of the last survivors of the Great Assembly. He used to say: On three things the world is sustained: on the Torah, on the (Temple) service, and on deeds of loving kindness. 3. Antigonus of Sokho received the Torah from Shim^con the Righteous. He used to say: Be not like servants who minister unto their master for the sake of receiving a reward, but be like servants who serve their master not upon the condition of receiving a reward; and let the fear of Heaven be upon you."[13]

Most of the *Mishnah* is transmitted without attribution (*stam*). This usually indicates that many sages taught so, or that Yehudah Ha-Nasi ruled so. The *halakhic* ruling usually follows that view. Sometimes, however, it appears to be the opinion of a single Sage, and

---

[13] *Pirke Avot* 1:1.

the view of the Sages collectively is given separately. Nevertheless, the *Talmud* records a tradition that unattributed statements of the law represent the views of Rabbi Meir (*Babylonian Talmud,* Sanhedrin 86a), which supports the theory (by Rav Sherira Gaon) that he was the author of an earlier collection. For this reason, the few passages that actually say "this is the view of Rabbi Meir" represent cases where the author intended to present Rabbi Meir's view as a "minority opinion" not representing the accepted law. There have been a few additions since Rabbi Yehudah Ha-Nasi, in particular passages that cite him or his grandson, Rabbi Yehudah Nesiʾah; in addition, the *Mishnah* at the end of Tractate *Sotah* refers to the period after Rabbi's death. Because of the proliferation of earlier versions, it was deemed too difficult to retract anything already released, and therefore a second version of certain laws was released. The *Talmud* refers to these differing versions as *Mishnah Rishonah* ("First *Mishnah*")[14] and *Mishnah Aḥaronah* ("Later *Mishnah*"). The Talmudic scholar David Hoffman (1843–1921) suggested that *Mishnah Rishonah* actually refers to texts from earlier Sages upon which Rabbi based his *Mishnah.* There are also references to the "*Mishnah* of Rabbi ʿAkiva," though this may simply mean his teachings in general.

The *Mishnah* uses the term *halakhah* to designate authoritative traditions (Peʾah 2:6, Orlah 3:9, Yevamot 8:3) and accepted practices (Nazir 7:4, Bava Kama 3:9, ʿEduyot 1:5, Menaḥot 4:3, Nidah 4:3). A halakhic dichotomy is the one between "forbidden" (*asur*) and "permitted" (*mutar*). For example, the *Mishnah* may categorize sexual relations between two individuals under certain circumstances as permitted, and under other circumstances as forbidden. While eating on the Day of Atonement (*Yom Kippur*) is certainly forbidden, Tannaitic *halakhah* lists certain exceptions to this rule and even requires children under a certain age to eat. Similarly, the *halakhah* permits heating food on the Sabbath under certain circumstances.

---

[14] David Hoffman, *Mishnah Rishonah: Die erste Mischna und die Controversen der Tannaim, von D. Hoffmann; aus Anlass seines 70-jährigen Geburtstages namens seiner Schüler ins Hebräische übers. von Samuel Grünberg* (Jerusalem, 1967). (Hebrew)

Rabbinic commentaries on the *Mishnah* were redacted as the *Gemara*, which, coupled with the *Mishnah*, comprise the Talmuds, i.e., the *Jerusalem Talmud* and the *Babylonian Talmud*.[15] For example, *Mishnah*, Bava Metziʿa 7:1 teaches the following: "If a man hired laborers and ordered them to work early in the morning and late at night, he cannot compel them to work early and late if it is not the custom in that place." The *Gemara* (*Babylonian Talmud, Bava Metẓiʿa* 83a) comments:

> "Is it not obvious [that an employer cannot demand a change from the local custom]? The case in question is where the employer gave them a higher wage than was normal. In that case, it might be argued that he could then say to them, The reason I gave you a higher wage than is normal is so that you will work early in the morning and late at night. So the law tells us that the laborers may reply: The reason that you gave us a higher wage than is normal is for better work [not longer hours]."

The first printed edition of the *Mishnah* was published in Naples in 1492 by Soncino. There have been many subsequent editions, including the late nineteenth century Vilna edition, and the Albeck edition in the twentieth century. As well as being printed on its own, the *Mishnah* is included in all editions of the *Babylonian* and *Jerusalem Talmuds*. Among the notable commentaries are the one by Maimonides (Spain, 1138–1204, Egypt), who condensed the associated Talmudic debates, and offered his own conclusions in a number of undecided issues. His introduction to chapter ten of tractate Sanhedrin enumerates the Thirteen Fundamental Beliefs of Judaism:

1. The existence of God;
2. His unity;
3. Incorporeality;
4. His eternity;
5. God alone is the object of worship;

---

[15] Jacob Neusner, "The formation of rabbinic Judaism: from the Mishnah's philosophy to the Talmud's religion." In: *Or le-meʾir* (ed. Shamir Yona; Beer Sheva: Ben Gurion University of the Negev Press, 2010), 121–41, explains how Judaism was transformed by the *Mishnah*.

6. Revelation through His prophets;
7. The preeminence of Moses among the Prophets;
8. God's law was given on Mount Sinai;
9. The immutability of the Torah as God's law;
10. God's foreknowledge of the actions of human beings;
11. God rewards and punishes;
12. The coming of the Messiah;
13. Resurrection.

Rabbi Samson of Sens (France, c. 1150–1230) composed a *Mishnah* commentary on some tractates, which is interwoven with his commentary on the *Tosefta*. Rabbi Ovadiah ben Abraham of Bertinoro (Italy, c. 1445–1515) utilized the work of Maimonides and included Talmudic material. Yomtov Lipman Heller (Bavaria, 1578–1654, Poland) wrote a commentary called *Tosafot Yom Tov,* containing detailed glosses. *Tiferet Yisra'el* is a commentary by Rabbi Israel Lipschitz (Germany, 1782–1860). The commentary by Rabbi Pinḥas Kehati (Israel, 1910–1976) is written in Modern Hebrew and based on classical and contemporary works; his commentary is designed to make the *Mishnah* widely accessible.

Many modern historians have focused on the time of the formation of the *Mishnah*. Further questions are directed at the stages and the timeframe of the *Mishnah*'s redaction. Are the Mishnaic tractates based upon sources dating from Rabbi Yehudah Ha-Nasi's lifetime? Or is the Mishnaic text composed of earlier material, or, in the alternative, comprising later sources?[16] In response to these textual problems, modern scholars have adopted a number of different approaches. Some scholars maintain that there has been far-reaching editorial reshaping of the textual material in the *Mishnah* and in the Talmuds. Since there are no external sources to corroborate the *Mishnah*, they maintain that one cannot confirm the exact date of most statements, halakhic decisions, and narratives. Additionally, the authorship of the *Mishnah* cannot be ascertained

---

[16] David Weiss Halivni, "Sof hora'ah — the end of teaching what?" *Educational Deliberations: Studies in Education Dedicated to Shlomo (Seymour) Fox* (eds. M. Nisan and O. Schremer; Jerusalem: Keter, 2005), 76–83.

with absolute certainty.[17] Questions pertaining to the theology expressed in the *Mishnah*[18] and the different rabbinic schools in the different sections of the *Mishnah* have also been raised.[19] David Kraemer thinks that the *Mishnah* has been influenced and formed by post-Mishnaic redactors; nevertheless, the *Mishnah* contains sources which can be identified.[20] The *Mishnah*[21] points to Sinai as the origin of the *Mishnah*'s traditions and the chain of tradition from Sinai ends with named individuals found in the *Mishnah*.

Talmud

Talmud is the title of two works which are the product of the Palestinian[22] (Land of Israel) and Babylonian rabbinic schools during the Amoraic period, which extended from the third to the fifth century CE. One of these compilations is entitled *Talmud Yerushalmi* (*Jerusalem Talmud*) and the other *Talmud Bavli* (*Babylonian Talmud*). The authoritative body of Jewish law and non-legal texts accumulated over a period of seven centuries (c. 200 BCE – c. 500 CE) in the Land of Israel and Babylonia. The word *Talmud* derives from the

---

[17] Baruch M. Bokser, *Post Mishnaic Judaism in Transition: Samuel on Berakhot and the Beginnings of the Gemara* (Atlanta: Scholars Press, 1980), researches the evolution of Mishnaic statements by a Rabbi.

[18] Jacob Neusner, *Judaism: The Evidence of the Mishnah* (Chicago: University of Chicago Press, 1981), an early religious studies approach to the *Mishnah*, focusing upon theology.

[19] Joel Gereboff, *Rabbi Tarfon, the tradition, the man, and early Rabbinic Judaism* (Missoula, MT: Scholars Press, 1979), a study of this Rabbi who lived between the destruction of the Second Temple (70 CE) and the fall of Bethar (135 CE) during the Bar Kokhba War. Gary Porton, *The Traditions of Rabbi Ishmael* (Leiden: E.J. Brill, 1982), the Mishnaic contributions of one of the prominent leaders of the first generation of the *Tannaim*.

[20] David C. Kraemer, "The Mishnah," *The Cambridge History of Judaism* IV (2006) 299–315, a useful overview.

[21] Avot 1.

[22] The Jewish revolts against the Romans in the early centuries of the CE resulted in the forced dispersal of much of the Jewish population from Jerusalem and Judea; Jerusalem was renamed *Aelia Capitolina* and Judea was renamed *Syria Palestina*.

Hebrew root *l-m-d* ("study" or "teach"). The *Talmud* incorporates the *Mishnah* and the rabbinical interpretations of the *Mishnah*, known as the *Gemara*. For many centuries, the Jerusalem (or "Palestinian") *Talmud (Talmud Yerushalmi)* was largely neglected and the term *Talmud* came to be applied exclusively to the *Babylonian Talmud*. When the *Talmud* was censored by Christian censors in sixteenth century Europe, they almost consistently utilized the word *Gemara* for "Talmud." The "Oral Law," believed to be given to Moses on Mount Sinai, was codified in the Mishnah c. 200 CE — as mentioned above — while the *Gemara* presents the discussions during the following two centuries in the Land of Israel and the following three centuries in Babylonia.

The Talmudic period is divided into two periods, that of the *Mishnah* and that of the *Gemara*. *Halakhah*, which is understood to contain the sum of Jewish law, is based on a hierarchy of sources and traditions; the older the source, the greater its authority. Thus laws mentioned in the Bible have more authority than those mentioned in the *Mishnah*; laws in the *Mishnah* carry more weight than those found in the *Gemara*, laws quoted in the *Gemara* are more authoritative than later halakhic decisions, and so on. In keeping with this division of authority, the Rabbis of the different periods were given different titles: the Rabbis of the *Mishnah* are called *Tannaim*, those who teach; those of the *Talmud* are called *Amoraim*, those who explain.[23] The *Mishnah* was devoted almost exclusively

---

[23] The rabbinic interpreters of the Hebrew Bible and Jewish law referred to as *Amoraim* succeeded the *Tannaim* ("*Mishnah* teachers"). The designation *Amora* means "speaker" or "interpreter," the *Amoraim* are mainly viewed as undertaking the enormous task of interpreting and deriving *halakhah* (legal decisions) from the *Mishnah* and material not included in it (*beraitot*). Sometimes a clear tension exists between the *Mishnah* and Amoraic traditions due to different historical or socio-economic circumstances. The *Amoraim* were active between c. 220 CE (the traditional date of the redaction of the *Mishnah*) and 360 or 370 CE in the Land of Israel, and between 220 and approximately 500 CE in Babylonia. Already in late antiquity the *Amoraim* were viewed as being distinct from *Tannaim*, e.g., Rabbi Levi and Rabbi Simon (*Jerusalem Talmud,* Berakhot 1:1, 2c; *Babylonian Talmud*, ʿEruvin 7a; *Babylonian Talmud,* Sanhedrin 6a, 33a).The state-

to *halakhah* and contains only the end result of rabbinic debate and discussion; the arguments, the proofs, and the lengthy discussion of supporting biblical texts are in most instances absent. While the *Mishnah* is the preeminent collection of rabbinic statements from its period, it is not the only one. The method of studying the Oral Law was preserved in *Midrash Halakhah*, which refers to the rabbinic interpretations of biblical legal texts. Many of the rabbinic statements of law and biblical exegesis were not included in the *Mishnah* and in *Midrash Halakhah*. These statements are called *beraitot*. A collection of these *beraitot*, called the *Tosefta*, parallels the structure and format of the *Mishnah*. Yet even the *Tosefta* is not a complete compilation of all the rabbinic statements that were not included in the *Mishnah*. Innumerable *beraitot* were preserved in the *Gemara*, in particular in a non-canonical tractate of the *Babylonian Talmud*, *Derekh Eretz Rabbah*.

While the Land of Israel was the preeminent spiritual center of Judaism in the Mishnaic period, a second center was rapidly gaining prominence. In the three centuries following the redaction of the *Mishnah*, Rabbis throughout the Land of Israel and Babylonia analyzed, debated, and discussed that work. These discussions form the *Gemara*. Jews had lived in Babylonia since the exile following the destruction of the First Temple by the Babylonians in 586 BCE. By the time Rabbi Yehudah Ha-Nasi organized the *Mishnah*, the Babylonian academies were gaining influence. As a result, the *Gemara* developed separately in the two centers, the Land of Israel and Babylonia.

---

ments of the *Amoraim* constitute most of the attributed material in the Talmuds and the Amoraic midrash-compilations. The *Amoraim* are divided into generations of scholars: first generation (c. 230–250 CE), e.g., among the earliest *Amoraim* in Israel were Rabbi Yoḥanan and Shimʿon ben Lakish, while the first Babylonian *Amoraim* were Abba Arika, also referred to as Rav, and Shmuʾel; second generation (c. 250–290 CE); third generation (c. 290–320 CE); fourth generation (c. 320–350 CE); fifth generation (c. 350–371 CE); sixth generation (c. 371–427); seventh generation (c. 427–460); eighth generation (c. 460–500 CE). Amoraic academies were located in Tiberias, Sepphoris, Cæsarea, and other places in Israel and in Nehardea, Sura, and Pumbedita in Babylonia.

The *Babylonian Talmud* provides an insight into the debates and the discussions concerning a statement from the *Mishnah*, a biblical text, or a point of law, even though the *Talmud* contains the statements of Rabbis spanning several centuries. The editors expanded the discussions by combining material which originated in different academies or in different centuries. The primary purpose of the discussions is to elucidate the *Mishnah* text. The structure of the *Talmud* follows that of the *Mishnah*, in which six orders (*sedarim*) of general subject matter are divided into 60 or 63 tractates (*masekhtot*) of more focused subject compilations, though not all tractates have *Gemara*. Each tractate is divided into chapters (*perakim*) that are numbered and provided with titles, usually using the first one or two words in the first *Mishnah* statement. Each *perek* will contain several *Mishnah* statements with their accompanying exchanges that form the components of the *Gemara*; the name for a passage of *Gemara* is a *Sugya*. This discursive unit may also include a *Baraita* (Tannaitic statement) or *Tosefta*; it will typically comprise a detailed proof-based elaboration of a Mishnaic statement, whether halakhic or aggadic. A *Sugya* may extend beyond the subject of the *Mishnah*. The *Sugya* uses specific expressions that help to divide it into components, usually including a statement, a question on the statement, an answer, a proof for the answer or a refutation of the answer with its own proof. Thus the analysis of a Mishnaic passage and the subsequent discussion take the form of questions and answers, which sometimes appear anonymously, though more often the speaker's name (a Rabbi, a fictitious interlocutor, a historical person, a Samaritan, or another person) is mentioned. Exchanges between two (frequently anonymous and sometimes metaphorical) disputants were created or recorded; occasionally, the disputants were termed the *makshan* (questioner) and *tartzan* (answerer). Another important function of *Gemara* is to identify the correct biblical basis for a given law presented in the *Mishnah* and the logical process connecting one with the other; this activity was known as *Talmud* long before the existence of the *Talmud* as a text. Typically, the discussion then proceeds to discovery of the biblical verse or verses which are the source of the law under review. The next step is to compare and contrast the *Mishnah* with similar texts from other Mishnaic passages or from a *baraita*. In harmonizing the *Mishnah* with a *baraita*, the *Gemara* sometimes claims that the *Mishnah* is missing a detail, the insertion of which changes the meaning of the

Mishnah, thus removing the conflict between the two texts. Since the *Amoraim* were not allowed to disagree with an accepted law from the *Mishnah*, the *Mishnah* is sometimes used as the basis for attacking a position held by an *Amora*. If the *Mishnah* statement is an anonymous one, the *Amora* attributes it to a particular *Tanna*, while he himself sides with a different *Tanna* on this point of law. There are extensive debates in the *Gemara* about purely theoretical matters, such as the sacrifices or the Temple, which by then was no longer in existence. Sometimes, the *Gemara* discusses at great length opinions which are not accepted as law. Intermixed with the legal debates are large sections of *Midrash* (interpretations of sections of the biblical text), rabbinic stories about biblical characters and about the Rabbis, medical advice, science, ethics, philosophical debates, dream interpretations, historical information, magic, fairy tales, theology, demonology, and many additional topics.

While the starting-point of the *Gemara* discussions is the analysis of the *Mishnah*, the end point is the decision as to what is to be accepted as law. Very often, a new principle of law is established along with the final legal decision. On occasion there is even debate as to which opinion is to be accepted as normative practice. Not every *Sugya* comes to a conclusive decision on the law. Some end with the word *teku* — an acronym meaning that the problem appears insoluble and that the prophet Elijah will resolve it when he returns to earth to announce the coming of the Messiah.

The political, social, and economic milieu in the Land of Israel deteriorated more rapidly than in Babylonia. Thus the Rabbis were forced once again to commit the Oral Law to writing. By 425 CE, the first edition of the *Talmud* (*Mishnah* and *Gemara*) began to circulate. Since it was the product of the academies in the Land of Israel it was called the *Talmud de-Venei Maʿarava* (*Talmud* of the Western People). In later generations, it was called *Talmud Yerushalmi* (*Jerusalem Talmud*). Despite its name, the *Jerusalem Talmud* was not created by a rabbinical school in Jerusalem. During the period it represents, the Jewish population was concentrated in the northern half of the country. Thus the *Jerusalem Talmud* was edited over a period of two hundred years in the rabbinical academies of Caesarea, Sepphoris, and Tiberias. Traditionally, this *Talmud* was thought to have been redacted in c. 350 CE by Rav Muna and Rav Yossi in the Land of Israel. Its final redaction probably belongs to the end of the fourth century, but the individual scholars who brought it to its present form cannot be determined with absolute certainty. By this time Christianity had become the state religion of the Roman Empire and Jerusalem the holy city of Christianity. In 325 CE Constantine, the first Christian emperor, declared that Christianity should have nothing in common with Judaism, and Jews became outcasts. It is believed that the compilers of the *Jerusalem Talmud* consequently lacked the time to produce a work of the quality they had intended, since the extant text of the *Jerusalem Talmud* is incomplete and not as elaborate as the text of the *Babylonian Talmud*. The apparent cessation of work on the *Jerusalem Talmud* in the fifth century has been associated with the decision of Theodusius II in 425 CE to suppress the Jewish institution of the Patriarchate and put an end to the practice of formal ordination of rabbinic scholars. Collecting the textual material is attributed to the third-century *Amora* Rabbi Yoḥanan bar Nappaḥa, although the final redaction was completed long after his time.

The *Jerusalem Talmud*, which is only about a third the size of the *Babylonian Talmud*, does not include *Gemara* on the entire *Mishnah*. There is no *Gemara* for the last two orders of the *Mishnah*, i.e., *Kodashim* (laws of the Temple and the sacrifices) and *Toharot* (laws of ritual impurity). Some modern scholars have tried to prove the existence of a *Jerusalem Talmud* text for these two orders, but their arguments are considered inconclusive. On the other hand, the *Jerusalem Talmud* does include *Gemara* on the entire first division of the *Mishnah*, *Zeraᶜim*, dealing with agricultural laws. Despite the destruction of the Second Temple in 70 CE, which had a close connection to the land through the agricultural laws and sacrifices, the Jews in the Land of Israel still observed those agricultural laws that were not directly connected to the Temple (including laws of tithes and priestly dues). Thus the laws contained in the Order *Zeraᶜim* were studied in the rabbinic academies for their relevance to the land.

The *Gemara* of the *Jerusalem Talmud* is written in a Galilean dialect of Western Aramaic. A small amount of Hebrew is also present, along with some Latin and Greek, much of which appears in corrupt form. On the whole, the discussions are short and incisive. Approximately one-sixth of the *Jerusalem Talmud* deals with nonhalakhic matters. The reason for this may be the development of separate anthologies of *Midrash* (e.g., *Bereshit Rabbah*). The Rabbis studying in the academies in the Land of Israel did not live in a vacuum. There was constant movement of teachers and students between these academies and those in Babylonia. Despite the constant cross-fertilization of ideas and legal opinions, the *Jerusalem Talmud* was an attempt to preserve the proceedings of the academies in Israel before they were lost to posterity because of the rapidly deteriorating political situation in the country. While the Rabbis labored hastily in Tiberias to produce the first complete *Talmud*, the Rabbis in Babylonia were still debating the law.

The first known commentary on the *Jerusalem Talmud* is by Rabbi Solomon Sirillo, written in the Land of Israel c. 1530. Solomon Sirillo frequently offers better readings than those of (later) printed texts. At about the same time, another scholar, Rabbi Eleʿazar Azikri of Safed, composed an extensive commentary (*Sefer Ḥaredim*) on a number of tractates, some of which are to be found in the Vilna edition of the *Jerusalem Talmud*. As the Babylonian *Geonim* declared the *Babylonian Talmud* authoritative, the *Jerusalem Talmud* was long neglected. Rav Saadiah Gaon (c. 906–1006) was one of the few authorities to quote it in his responsa. It was, however, studied in Israel, North Africa, and southern Italy. Medieval Spanish talmudists, beginning with Maimonides, cited it far more frequently than their Franco-German contemporaries. The *aggadah* from the *Jerusalem Talmud* was published separately in 1590 by Rabbi Samuel Yafeh Ashkenazi. In the seventeenth century Rabbi Joshua Beneviste wrote a commentary based upon Sirillo. Rabbi David Fränkel (Germany, 18th cent.) was the author of an extensive commentary on the Orders *Zeraʿim and Moʿed*, entitled *Korban ʿEdah*. The most comprehensive commentary, covering the entire work, is by Rabbi Moses Margolies, a Lithuanian talmudist (d. 1780). The commentary is divided into *Pene Mosheh* and *Marʾeh ha-Penim*. The former is a running commentary; the latter a series of novellae. The author was the first to make use of the *Tosefta* in interpreting the *Jerusalem Talmud*. In the twentieth century, academic study of the *Jerusalem Talmud* included Saul Lieberman, Louis Ginzberg, Jacob Neusner, and Adin Steinsalz. A preliminary English translation was edited by Jacob Neusner,[24] a synoptic edition based upon extant manuscript material and early printed editions of the entire *Jerusalem Tamud*,[25] as well as a translation into German, is in progress in Germany.

The *Babylonian Talmud (Talmud Bavli)* is very different from the *Jerusalem Talmud*. Its *Gemara* is Hebrew and Eastern (Babylonian) Aramaic and Greek and Latin terms are used as well; additionally, there are Persian and other loanwords. The discussions in the *Babylonian Talmud* are more expansive and more tangential material is included. Only about a third of the *Gemara* relates to *halakhah*, while almost two-thirds are *Midrash* and *aggadah*. The *Babylonian Talmud* contains *Gemara* on the first tractate (*Berakhot*) in the *Mishnah*, Order *Zeraᶜim*, and addresses the laws of prayer, but since there was no obligation to observe the agricultural laws outside the Land of Israel, it contains no *Gemara* on the rest of the Order *Zeraᶜim*, which is devoted to those laws. On the other hand, it contains *Gemara* on each of the books in the Order *Kodashim* (laws pertaining to sacrifices), despite the fact that after the destruction of the Jerusalem Temple the material had become theoretical. The *Babylonian Talmud* has *Gemara* on only one tractate in the last Order, *Toharot* (laws of ritual impurity), namely, tractate *Niddah* addressing the laws relating to menstruating women.

The *Mishnah* text which appears in the *Babylonian Talmud* includes many variants from that in the *Jerusalem Talmud*. Scholars disagree about the sources of these variant readings. Some think that they derive from earlier or later editions of the *Mishnah*, with the *Jerusalem Talmud* using a later, updated version of the *Mishnah*. Alternatively, the Babylonian version may reflect the different way the *Mishnah* was studied in the Babylonian academies (i.e., Nehardea, Nisibis, Mahoza, Pumbedita, and Sura) during late antiquity (third to fifth centuries CE). The Rabbis in Babylonia were more critical of the *Mishnah* text and emended it. However, only

---

[24] *The Talmud of the Land of Israel: A Preliminary Translation and Explanation* (ed. Jacob Neusner; Chicago Studies in the History of Judaism; Chicago: University of Chicago Press, 1982–1991).

[25] Peter Schäfer et al. (eds.), *Synopse zum Talmud Yerushalmi*, vols. 1– (Tübingen: Mohr/Siebeck, 1991–).

rarely are the variants so different that the resulting law is affected. The foundations of this process of analysis were laid by Rav, a disciple of Rabbi Judah Ha-Nasi. The two Talmuds differ significantly in language, style, content, scope and range of subject matter, date of redaction, and ultimately in the authority each has in matters of law.

Traditionally, it was held that the *Babylonian Talmud* was edited by Rav Ashi and Ravina. Rav Ashi was president of the Sura Academy from 375 to c. 427 CE. The work begun by Rav Ashi was completed by Ravina, who is traditionally regarded as the final Amoraic interpreter.[26] Accordingly, traditionalists argue that Ravina's death in 499 CE is the latest possible date for the completion of the redaction of the *Talmud*. This has now been questioned, since it is assumed that the process of editing and arranging the material took place in a number of stages over a period of several generations. It may have been the work of anonymous editors living after the death of Rav Ashi, who would have set the standards, and concluded the work. Even subsequently the later scholars, the *Savoraim*, did not hesitate to insert brief explanatory notes into the text. In the centuries after its final redaction, the Babylonian academies expanded and became more influential. As a result, less than two centuries after its completion, the *Geonim* used the *Babylonian Talmud* as the basis for their authoritative rulings. In the Geonic period, no need was felt for an extensive commentary on the *Talmud*, since generally its language and its *realia* were familiar. Therefore, with the exception of a commentary on the Order *Toharot* ascribed to Ḥai Gaon (Ḥai ben Sherira, 939–1038) and an interpretation of a Talmudic word or phrase here and there, no comprehensive commentaries were written in that period. The situation was different in both North Africa and in the Franco-German center of Judaism by the eleventh century. In neither place was Aramaic the spoken language, while *realia* were different. In the early eleventh century, Rabbenu Gershom ben Judah compiled a commentary on several tractates. This commentary comprises an anthology

---

[26] Richard Kalmin, "The post-Rav Ashi Amoraim: transition or continuity? A study of the role of the final generations of Amoraim in the redaction of the Talmud," *AJS Review* 11 (1986), 157–87.

of explanatory notes on the Talmudic text by a number of commentators. In the same period, R. Ḥananel ben Ḥushiel of Kairouan in Tunisia wrote a running commentary on most Talmudic tractates. There is evidence that his commentary covered the entire *Talmud*, but only parts are extant. He utilized the *Jerusalem Talmud* to illuminate the text of the *Babylonian Talmud*. His commentary is found in standard editions of the *Talmud*.

The commentary of Rashi (Rabbi Shlomo Yitzḥaki, France/Germany, 1040–1104) on most of the *Babylonian Talmud* (with the exception of a few tractates erroneously ascribed to him, e.g., *Taᶜanit* and *Moᶜed Katan*) remains unsurpassed for both its comprehensiveness and its clarity. Drawing on the traditions of the school of Rabbenu Gershom and his own teachers in Worms/Germany, where he had studied, he succeeded in illuminating obscure passages. From his commentary, it is evident that Rashi did not intend it for the beginning student, for he takes it for granted that its readers are familiar with the more common vocabulary of both Hebrew and Aramaic, although Rashi provides Hebrew synonyms for difficult Aramaic terms. Where a Hebrew synonym is not available, Rashi offers a French translation. Rashi's own pupils and relatives are the authors of the Tosafot, who clarify points in critical glosses. Rashi's commentary is printed on the inner margins of the pages of the *Talmud* and the Tosafot are on the outer margins.

Rabbenu Nissim ben Reʾuven Gerondi (Spain, fourteenth century) was the author of commentaries on several tractates (Shabbat, Pesaḥim, Betzah, Rosh Ha-Shanah, Yoma, Taᶜanit, Megillah, Sukkah, Ketubbot, Gittin, Kiddushin, Shevuᶜot, Avodah Zarah, Ḥullin, and Niddah), as well as novella on several tractates. The codifiers of Jewish law, Isaac Alfasi (1013–1103), Moses Maimonides (known by the acronym Rambam, Spain, 1138–1204, Egypt), Rabbi Asher ben Jehiel (known by the acronym Rosh and also as Asheri; c. 1250–1327) and Joseph Karo (Toledo, 1488–1575, Safed, Israel) determined the preeminence of the Babylonian Talmud as the halakhically accepted version of the Talmud.

Only a small number of manuscripts of the *Talmud* predating the 16th century are extant today, e.g., MS Munich of the Bavarian State Library. This is probably the result of the war waged by the Roman Catholic Church against the *Talmud*, which resulted in numerous burnings of the *Talmud*, e.g., 1242 in Paris. The Church continued with periodic attacks and burnings well into the 16th century. The first complete edition of the *Babylonian Talmud* was printed in Venice by the Christian publisher Daniel Bomberg in 1520–23. He also printed the *Jerusalem Talmud* shortly thereafter. Since then the *Talmud* has been published numerous times. An often quoted edition was published in Vilna before the turn of the nineteenth century. The first translation of the *Babylonian Talmud* into a European language (German) is that of Lazarus Goldschmidt (1897–1909). The Soncino Press in London published the first complete English translation, edited by Isidor Epstein (1935–1952). A new English translation was published under the editorship of Jacob Neusner.[27] A translation into Modern Hebrew is being undertaken by Rabbi Adin Steinsalz, who is simultaneously producing an English edition. The study of *Talmud* achieved such importance that the commandment of Torah study (Deut. 6:7 and Deut. 11:19) was interpreted to apply to *Talmud* study. To this day, *Talmud* study remains the primary occupation in rabbinic academies throughout the world.

Midrash

Whereas the *Mishnah* was interpreted in the Talmuds, a different interpretive approach of playful and creative discourse on the meaning of scriptural lemmata developed into the literary genre *Midrash*, which flourished in the first six centuries of the Common Era. In its constructed discussions, *Midrash* explicates multiple meanings of scriptural passages, which is one of its distinctive and characteristic elements. This polysemy seems to be based upon the underlying ideology of Midrashic exegesis; this polysemy is a literary creation based upon the redactional juxtaposition of conflicting views, since — similar to the *Talmud* — all opinions are recorded as a conversation between Rabbis.

Midrash is the particular mode of interpreting the Hebrew Bible that was developed by the Rabbis of late antiquity in the Land of Israel. *Midrash* rendered Scripture relevant to the needs of a spe-

---

[27] Jacob Neusner (ed.), *The Babylonian Talmud: A Translation and Commentary*, 22 Vols. (Peabody, MA: Hendrickson Publishers, 2005).

cific period in time. Definitions of *Midrash,* the scope of Midrashic activity, and its applicability to multiple interpretive strategies are widely disputed among scholars. There were three major approaches to the Hebrew Bible in late antiquity that often overlapped: (1) translation; (2) rewriting or paraphrase; (3) commentary; (3a) *Midrash* as a subgroup of commentaty. One might want to add a fourth approach, the appropriation of a text that was in the possession of one group by other groups, in order to create a new (religious) identity. *Midrash* is certainly a sub-genre of rabbinic literature; the difference between some Bible commentaries and *Midrash* is in the spatial arrangement. Commentary is line-by-line, whereas *Midrash* "weaves" its exegesis of single biblical lemmata into coherent statements. Rabbinic *Midrash* as a literary genre is dependent upon formalistic and socio-economic features, as well as upon its anonymous authors who embody rabbinic practice; these conditions determine the limits of *Midrash* in its halakhic, aggadic or homiletical expressions.

INNER-BIBLICAL INTERPRETATION

Midrash is often viewed as the exploration of God's plan for the Jewish people as recorded in the written text of the Hebrew Bible since God's speech is no longer audibly communicated.[28] The assumption that *Midrash* exists in the Bible relies upon the occurrence of the term *darash* (e.g., Gen. 25:22, Ezra 7:10) which has the twofold meaning of seeking and interpreting; although this term is related to the noun *Midrash*, its meaning shifted over time and within different biblical books. After the Exodus from Egypt, God and His voice dwelled in a sanctuary which subsequently evolved into the First Temple in Jerusalem. After the destruction of this Temple in 586 BCE the direct access to the words of God was largely lost. Instead, the text was to be found in a portable document, the Torah scroll.[29] Ezra the scribe, who was sent by the Persians from

[28] Michael Fishbane, *The Garments of Torah: Essays in Biblical Hermeneutics* (Bloomington: Indiana University Press, 1989).

[29] Jacob Neusner, *Torah: From Scroll to Symbol* (Atlanta: Scholars Press, 1988).

exile in Babylonia to Jerusalem in order to reestablish Judaism, did not receive direct communication from God but interpreted the scroll text. The origins of rabbinic *Midrash* may actually lie in the "enactment" of laws during the ensuing Second Temple period, since Ezra was the paradigm of a *sofer,* someone interpreting and teaching the law, as well as being a priest. The term *darash* in the Second Temple period denoted instruction rather than hermeneutic interpretation.

Two passages in the Hebrew Bible contain the term *Midrash*: *written in the Midrash of the prophet Iddo* (2 Chr. 13:22) and *written in the Midrash of the Book of the Kings* (2 Chr. 24:27). These passages have led to speculation that the Bible contained or utilized interpretations that are comparable to rabbinic *Midrash*. However, the term *Midrash* as utilized by the Chronicler refers to extra-biblical sources; we have no certainty what type of historical or interpretive texts these may have been. Inner-biblical interpretation occurred and was carried out within the biblical canon; these interpretations did become part of the Hebrew Scriptures in the form of comments, revisions, and rewritings of the text from one textual genre (e. g., the biblical law codes) into another genre (psalms or prophecies). However, there is no *Midrash* within the Bible; rabbinic *Midrash* is one of the late antique post-biblical texts that demonstrate an interpretive relationship to the Hebrew Bible.

One may note interpretive activity in the community at Qumran (Dead Sea Scrolls) as well as in the allegorical interpretation of the Bible by Philo of Alexandria. In particular, the genre of rewritten Bible (e.g., the *Genesis Apocryphon* and the *Temple Scroll* in the Dead Sea Scrolls) has been compared to *Midrash*. In this "parabiblical literature" the line between Scripture and its interpretive reading is fluid. The beginning of Midrashic activity is marked by a shift from priestly to non-priestly (i.e., rabbinic) authority. Further comparisons between pre-rabbinic and rabbinic interpretation, on the one hand, and between the so-called Tannaitic and Amoraic *Midrashim*, on the other hand, have demonstrated how certain characteristic features of *Midrash* developed at specific times and in specific contexts. For example, the term *Midrash* rarely appears in another rabbinic document, the *Mishnah*; on the few occasions that the term appears it denotes a teaching. The problem of distinguishing between the meaning given to a Hebrew term such as *Midrash* and the meaning it may have had in other late antique texts has not been fully explored.

The term *Midrash* that denotes the rabbinic method of Bible interpretation has its starting point in the canonical biblical text, and the Bible is cited in *Midrash*. Alternatively, *Midrash* may refer to individual exegetical pericopae and to the anthologies or works containing rabbinic exegetical statements.[30] Thus we find an ostensible *Midrash* on a biblical book, such as the Midrashic compilation *Bereshit Rabbah*, which is a work that contains a well-structured collection of exegetical rabbinic statements on lemmata from the biblical Book of Genesis. Furthermore, *Midrash* may also be found in works of rabbinic literature that are not called *Midrash*, notably the Targums, the Talmuds and medieval Bible commentaries. In short, the term *Midrash* denotes multiple phenomena; it may refer to the process of interpreting Scripture, the theology of its interpreters as well as the results of their interpretations.[31] *Midrash* is uniquely and distinctively rabbinic, finding its fullest expression in the interpretations collected in the classical Midrashic works compiled by Rabbis.

A major characteristic of *Midrash* is lemmatization (segmentation) of the biblical texts; rabbinic interpretation focused upon meaningful parts, such as a word, a letter, or sign in the Bible. Rabbinic interpretation highlights the multiple meanings of a sign of Scripture. An example of lemmatization and of rabbinic theology in *Midrash* is found in the following text that focuses upon the lemmata *in the beginning* and *amon* in Gen. 1:1.

> "*In the beginning* [*bereshit*][32] (Gen. 1:1). Rabbi Oshaya interpreted: *Then I was with Him as a nursling* [*amon*], *a source of delight every day,* [*rejoicing before Him at all times*][33] (Prov. 8:30).

Amon means 'tutor' [pedagogue].

---

[30] Gary G. Porton, "Definitions of *Midrash*." In: *Encyclopedia of Midrash*, Leiden: Brill, 2005), vol. 1, 520–34.

[31] Jacob Neusner, *Invitation to Midrash: The Workings of Rabbinic Bible Interpretation* (Atlanta: Scholars Press, 1992).

[32] Transcription of the Hebrew term.

[33] Continuation of the biblical verse that is not cited in the rabbinic text.

> *Amon* means 'covered.'
>
> *Amon* means 'hidden.'
>
> And there are some who say,
>
> *Amon* means 'great.'
>
> *Amon* means 'tutor,' as in the verse, *as an amon carries the suckling child* (Num. 11:12). *Amon* means 'covered,' as in the verse, *those who are covered in scarlet* (Lam 4:5). *Amon* means 'hidden,' as in the verse, *and he hid Hadassah* (Est. 2:7). *Amon* means 'great,' as it says, *are you better than No-Ammon* (Nah. 3:8)? This we translate: Are you better than Alexandria the Great, which is situated in the [Nile] delta? Another interpretation: *Amon* means 'artisan [*uman*].' The Torah declares, I was the artisan's tool that the Holy One, blessed be He, used [when he practiced His craft]. It is customary, when a human king builds a palace, he does not build it out of his own head, but he employs an architect [*uman*]. Even the architect does not build it from his head, but he uses plans and blueprints in order to know how to plan the rooms and the doorways. So, too, the Holy One, blessed be He, looked into the Torah and created the world. Thus the Torah said, *By means of the beginning did God create* (Gen. 1:1). And the word for 'beginning' refers only to the Torah, as it says: The *Lord acquired me at the beginning* [*reshit*] *of His course* (Prov. 8:22)."[34]

This Midrashic passage contains several different interpretations of one biblical lemma, *amon*, before it returns to interpretations of *bereshit* (Gen. 1:1). The representation of the content of the lexical item *amon* utilizes some knowledge from other scriptural verses, and it enables the reader to decide which properties are essential to the overall statement of the *Midrash.* As usual, the *Midrash* uses the method of focusing upon certain lemmata which are linked by the same Hebrew root [*Amn*] and its many possible meanings. The words of the *Midrash* have to be read accumulatively and from the bottom up. Every single mention of *amon* and its surprising new

---

[34] *Bereshit Rabbah* 1:1.

meaning has to be considered. Against the usual understanding of *amon* as "nursling" the *Midrash* establishes the opposite meaning of *amon* as "tutor" from another scriptural passage. The result is that the Torah, according to this Midrashic interpretation, can accommodate both of these terms as well as the other meanings of *amon*. Every single meaning is applicable in the Midrashic passage. Additionally, the many uses of the Hebrew root *Amn* of *amon* and the comprehensive aspect of this *Midrash* may lead the knowledgeable reader to the term *Amen*, which is the worshipers' response. This aspect includes that the Torah is covered in garments, when it is carried like a "nursling" (small child) during the Torah procession and that the Torah is not immediately visible; "hidden" and "covered" may mean that the Torah is stored in the ark and that it is covered by its "garments." On the level of Midrashic interpretation, the sense is that the linguistic signs of the Torah have to be uncovered, i.e., interpreted. On a more metaphorical level, it is obvious that the Torah had to be revealed to the people of Israel because it was hidden; it was taught and written and ultimately great wisdom evolved from it.

A major theological concern of the Rabbis was that the Torah had to be differentiated from anything foreign, in particular from anything "Egyptian;" thus the Torah is greater than No-Ammon, a location in Egypt. By virtue of the hermeneutic strategy of "updating" (contemporizing) the *Midrash* changes this location to the Hellenistic Egyptian metropolis of Alexandria. This method of updating or translating brings into view a better-known or contemporary city, Alexandria, a center of wisdom and learning of the Hellenistic/Roman world. The hermeneutic strategy thus enables the formation of a theological statement: the Torah given to Israel is greater and contains more wisdom than the greatest source of wisdom of the nations.[35]

The artisan part of the above *Midrash* demonstrates that the Torah was the plan for the world that was to be created. This is the so-called dogma of "the pre-existence of the Torah," which is an-

[35] Rivka Ulmer, *Egyptian Cultural Icons in Midrash* (Studia Judaica, Forschungen zur Wissenschaft des Judentums 52; Berlin & New York: Walter de Gruyter, 2009).

other major theological expression of rabbinic Judaism. Additionally, it means that God is bound by the plan in the Torah, and if God is bound by the plan of the Torah, so much more will the Torah bind humans. The implication of the *mashal* method (interpretation in parables) is to show God's integrity and His plan for the world and for humanity. The essential, theological result of the hermeneutic strategies and the resulting reading is that *bereshit* ("in the beginning," Gen. 1:1) means that the world was created "with *reshit*" removing the temporal aspect and replacing it with wisdom. This is a theological proposition of the Midrashic unit, which could have been stated at the beginning of the unit, but, as is often the case in *Midrash*, the *Midrash* has to be read from the bottom up to gain this conceptual understanding of a sequential "order of things." The rabbinic text requires the reader to follow well-reasoned steps of analyses and "different" readings of a polysemic term, all of which are appropriate and valid.

From its infancy in the nineteenth century[36] the academic study of *Midrash* evolved into a specialized discipline within Jewish Studies in general and within rabbinics in particular. Major research into Midrashic literature was accomplished in the twentieth century; however, the discussion of the phenomenon *Midrash* continues to engage scholars from multiple disciplines demonstrating a diversity of approaches to *Midrash*. The methodological and philosophical approaches to *Midrash* changed significantly in Europe in the 1960's through the early1980's; these new methodologies utilized literary criticism, literary theory and models of comparative literature, as well as the science of textlinguistics and generative semantics. This was probably due to the fact that *Midrash* was studied at the university outside the confinements of religion. Concurrently, *Midrash* was approached as an expression of an essential element of Judaism.[37] After the initial rejections of European-based literary criticism in the study of *Midrash* (and of rabbinic literature in gen-

[36] Leopold Zunz, *Die gottesdienstlichen Vorträge der Juden historisch entwickelt … 1892* (repr. Piscataway, NJ: Gorgias, 2003), xxi–xxxviii (English introduction).

[37] James Kugel, "Two Introductions to *Midrash*," *Prooftexts* 3 (1983), 131–55.

eral) some scholars in the United States eventually followed this methodological stimulus,[38] and produced their own critical reading of *Midrash* as literature.[39] The literary-critical approach went beyond the previously assumed function of *Midrash* to fill in gaps in the biblical text. The term "intertextuality" was applied to *Midrash*; intertextuality means that interpreters utilize previous texts, adding material and editing the text, and that they drew upon a store of pre-existing or traditional ideas.[40] Additionally, feminist studies began to pay attention to *Midrash* and mined *Midrash* for the roles women were assigned in late antique Judaism.[41] Recent scholarship has focused upon cultural intersections, polemics, memory, and identity.[42]

The definition of *Midrash* has often focused upon the particularity of rabbinic hermeneutics. However, one may argue that many of the exegetical strategies that are found in *Midrash* were also utilized by other social groups that created interpretive texts. Thus the authors of *Midrash* may be viewed in contrast to other exegetes, who attempted to find definite scriptural meanings, whereas the Rabbis are considered to be creative in their approaches to Scripture as an endlessly generative source of truth, a divine text that accepts a plurality of human interpretations. Whereas Christian interpreters adopted Hellenistic modes of literary production such as authorship, the texts of the rabbinic interpreters are collected in anonymously edited works such as *Bereshit Rabbah*. *Midrash* accomplishes the structuring of arguments in well-ordered reasoning in

---

[38] Geoffrey Hartman and Sanford Budick (eds.), *Midrash and Literature*, New Haven: Yale University Press, 1986).

[39] David Stern, *Midrash and Theory. Ancient Jewish Exegesis and Contemporary Literary Studies* (Evanston: Northwestern University Press, 1996).

[40] Daniel Boyarin, *Intertextuality and the Reading of Midrash* (Bloomington: Indiana University Press, 1990).

[41] Judith Baskin, *Midrashic Women: Formation of the Feminine in Rabbinic Literature* (Hanover, NH: University Press of New England, 2002).

[42] David W. Nelson and Rivka Ulmer (eds.), *Re-presenting Texts: Jewish and Black Biblical Interpretation: Proceedings of the 2010 and 2011 SBL Midrash Sections* (Piscataway, NJ: Gorgias Press, 2013).

which the Torah serves as a discussion partner and occasionally is assigned its own pronoun: "it says."[43]

In order to address the place of *Midrash* within the rabbinic interpretive tradition, the concepts of the Written and the Oral Torah as well as the so-called "chain of tradition" have to be considered (see above). One important rabbinic assumption in *Midrash* is that the Oral Torah, the authoritative interpretation of the Written Torah, was given to Moses on Sinai; this assumption would render the Oral Torah as coexistent with the Written Torah. The chain of tradition, which provides a list of the tradents of the Oral Torah from Moses to the Rabbis, established the hermeneutic link between revelation at Sinai and rabbinic interpretation.

In addition to the rabbinic form of interpretation as recorded in the *Mishnah*, a different approach to *halakhah* emerged in the halakhic *Midrashim*. The question remains open, whether the Sages at the time of the Second Temple utilized Midrashic methods as found in later Midrashic works, such as *Sifra* (probably second half of the third century) and *Sifre* (probably after the middle of the third century), and derived *halakhot* (legal statements) from Scripture. *Sifra* quotes from other rabbinic works, *Mishnah* and *Tosefta*, and it establishes that laws in the *Mishnah* derive from Scripture. Since the Pharisees utilized the Oral Torah to support their authority, *Midrash* may have been the earlier method of deriving the *halakhah*. On the other hand, if the Mishnaic method, i.e., rarely citing Scripture in free-standing *mishnayot*, preceded *Midrash,* it could also support the position that *halakhah* was not originally derived from Scripture.

The Midrashic texts and works have been classified into different groups of texts, although there is an overlap between different texts. It is therefore difficult to differentiate Midrashic works into the standard classifications such as halakhic (legal), aggadic (narrative), exegetical or homiletic, because the texts are not homogenous; furthermore, it is difficult to date Midrashic texts because they grew by accretion and because the material is intercon-

---

[43] Rivka Ulmer, "Discourse in *Midrash*: Textual Strategy and the Use of Personal Pronouns in Halakhic *Midrash*," *Approaches to Ancient Judaism, N.S.* 13 (1998), 51–70.

nected. In addition to the above-mentioned halakhic *Midrashim* (e.g., *Sifra*) there are "non-halakhic" Midrashim, which may include the Amoraic *Midrashim* (e.g., *Bereshit Rabbah*; *Eikhah Rabbah*, *Esther Rabbah*, c. 400–500), as well as the "post-Amoraic *Midrashim*" (e.g., *Pesikta de-Rav Kahana*; *Ruth Rabbah*, c. 500–640; *Midrash Tehillim*; *Kohelet Rabbah*, c. 640–900; *Devarim Rabbah*; parts of *Shemot Rabbah*, c. 775–900). These texts consist of two very fluid and often overlapping categories. The first category comprises the aggadic *Midrashim* (e.g., *Bemidbar Rabbah*; *Devarim Rabbah*) that display the discernible form of rabbinic *Midrash* (a scriptural lemma, a Midrashic operation and a Midrashic statement) or the literary form of the rabbinic homily.[44] The rabbinic homily contains Midrashic forms that interpret the lectionary verse of the synagogue reading, and it has a concluding homiletic unit (e.g., *Vayikra Rabbah*, *Pesikta Rabbati*, *Tanḥuma*). All of these works are referred to as the "classical Midrashim." The second category comprises mainly medieval *Midrashim*[45] that are somewhat reminiscent of the previously mentioned exegetical and homiletic *Midrashim* but show few of the formal Midrashic characteristics (e.g., *Aggadat Bereshit*, *Midrash Konen*, *Petirat Moshe*, *Midrash Temurah*, *Midrash Tadshe*).

Midrash may be viewed as a genre of its own kind that cannot be compared to other bodies of literature. As a literary genre *Midrash* is defined by the social group that created and used it. Furthermore, a literary genre constitutes a series of texts that exhibit a coherent and recurring configuration of literary features involving structure, content, and function. Additionally, the determination of the genre *Midrash* in its social function offers a particular mode of expression, and it provides the basis for *Midrash* to become "ethicizing" and "theologizing." *Midrash* may be a performatory literary genre which was established for teaching and transmission purposes. Economic factors, such as the agricultural society in the Land of Israel, as well as trading and professional activities, such as tax collecting, shifted and influenced the purposes of late antique rabbinic

---

[44] Arnold Goldberg, "Form-analysis of *Midrash* Literature as a Method of Description," *Journal of Jewish Studies* 36 (1985), 159–74.

[45] Jacob Elbaum, "From Sermon to Story; the Transformation of the Akedah," *Prooftexts* 6 (1986), 97–116.

writings. When the socio-economic and intellectual basis of the literary genre *Midrash* was lost in the Land of Israel and when Midrashic activity was transferred to the Diaspora, the genre and the interests of the social group that maintained *Midrash* changed. Based upon the socio-economic definition of literary genres, *Midrash* could be viewed as the rabbinic approach to the Hebrew Bible, while somewhat similar methods of interpretation are found in earlier (*Dead Sea Scrolls*) and in different texts (in the Greek of the *New Testament*). In Judaism, the hermeneutic tradition that began with biblical interpretation, if not earlier with inner-biblical exegesis, developed its distinctive hermeneutics in *Midrash. Midrash* is mainly used as a *terminus technicus* describing rabbinic interpretation of the Bible, because *Midrash* is a rabbinic genre that was first used by the Rabbis to denote their own method of interpreting the Hebrew Bible; by necessity, *Midrash* is related to Scripture and it presents itself formally as commentary.

Medieval *Midrash* continued to derive historical or ethical lessons from the Bible (or from the *Pseudepigrapha*) and attempted to imitate the ancient form of *Midrash.* Usually, there was a transition from "exegetical" and "aggadic" *Midrash* to medieval stories that relate to the Bible or were based upon tales from the Christian or Islamic milieus, which were the main cultures of the Jewish Diaspora. Historical factors contributed and conditioned the production of *Midrash* (e.g., *Midrash Lekaḥ Tov* on Songs 1:3 reflects the European martyrs of the Crusades). Another significant change that transpired during the Middle Ages was that frequently Midrashic works had a known author, e.g., *Bereshit Rabbati* was composed by Moshe Ha-Darshan from Narbonne (eleventh century).[46]

The social context of the community, and the theological threats present in the Land of Israel and in the Medieval Diaspora, necessitated that the creators of *Midrash* adapt a situation in the ancient past of the Bible to the more pressing concerns of the Diaspora. *Midrash* reacts to hermeneutically significant events and *Midrash* as a hermeneutic activity may have its own metahistorical

---

[46] Rivka Ulmer, "*Pesiqta Rabbati*: A Text Linguistic and Form-Analytical Analysis of the Rabbinic Homily," *Journal of Jewish Studies* 64 (2013), 64–97.

approach to the essential meaning of historical events. History is a part of the cultural memory transferred to the rabbinic interpreters and filtered into lessons about God and His involvement in Israel's history. In the distant past, Jerusalem, the capital of the southern Kingdom of Judah, survived an Assyrian siege staged by Sennacherib (in 702 BCE), unlike Samaria, the capital of the northern Kingdom of Israel, that had fallen some twenty years earlier. The survival of Jerusalem, according to Scripture, occurred at night when an angel of the Lord killed 185,000 men in Sennacherib's army. Thus the seemingly hopeless situation of King Hezekiah defending Jerusalem must have been God's plan. Perhaps Hezekiah was placed by God in this precarious situation to teach Hezekiah a lesson, since he abolished some of the "Lord's" cultic centers outside of Jerusalem (2 Kgs. 18:4). It is important to note that in rabbinic Judaism God and the Lord are the one and the same expression referring to a transcendent deity that acts in history. In this instance God's action in history was to bring down His angel to destroy the army of Sennacherib. It is important to emphasize that Sennacherib was punished through God's agent (an angel), not by God Himself (*Babylonian Talmud*, Sanhedrin 94b).

According to the Midrashic interpretation set forth below, Sennacherib's army was annihilated on the eve of Passover when King Hezekiah recited the Hallel Psalms (Ps. 113–118). In a Midrashic text the liturgical recital of the Hallel by Hezekiah and Israel is mentioned; the midrash states that this is a customary recital during Passover. In the applicable sections of the Bible only Hezekiah and Isaiah pray to God. In the midrash set forth below Israel, meaning all the Jewish people, including Hezekiah, recited the *Hallel* together. This insertion into the midrash may have reflected the contemporary liturgical practice at the time of *Shemot Rabbah* concerning the observance of Passover.

> "Israel and Hezekiah sat that night and recited the Hallel, since it was Passover, but they were terrified for fear that at any moment Jerusalem might fall at [Sennacherib's] hand. When they arose early in the morning to recite the *shema*ᶜ and pray, they found their enemies' dead corpses; that is the reason why God said to Isaiah: *Call his name Maher-shalal-hash-baz* [*hasten for spoil, hurry for plunder*] (Isa. 8:3), and he made haste to plunder their spoil. Another called him *Immanuel* [*God is with us*] (Isa.

> 7:14) that is, "I will be with him," as it says: *With him is an arm of flesh; but with us is the Lord our God* (2 Chron. 32:8)."[47]

The above Midrashic text points to a perceived difference between Sennacherib and Israel by utilizing the verse 2 Chron. 32:8 stating that Israel has God with them, whereas the enemy has only the power of a human being.

Another example of this type of metahistorical approach is found in a Midrashic interpretation that is part of a rabbinic homily for *Hanukkah*, a festival ordained by the Rabbis and not found in the Hebrew Bible; this festival has to be anchored in the Bible and rabbinic authority has to be confirmed:

> "Another interpretation: *The words of the wise are as goads* [*kadarbanot*] (Eccl. 12:11). Rabbi Berekhiah Ha-Kohen says, like a ball girls use, [*kadur shel banot*], which they pick up and throw about, this way and that. It is the same with the words of the wise: One Sage gives his view and another gives his."[48]

The ball game metaphor fits the general concerns of the Midrashic text, i.e., how to survive in the Diaspora and observe the laws pertaining to the festival of *Hanukkah*. The Midrashic passage offers a glimpse into rabbinic interpretive activity and how the social group that created *Midrash* positioned itself as the sole heirs to revelation. Words were tossed from Sinai during revelation like balls and now — that is in the present tense of the *Midrash* — words are tossed back and forth between the Rabbis who are interpreting Scripture. Interpretation is continuous, but it is subjected to the rules of a game.

The Rabbis of late antiquity and subsequent generations of Rabbis attempted to limit the number of hermeneutical rules in order to make Midrashic exegesis *finite* and limit its interpretations;[49] other ways of limiting *Midrash* include the circle of interpreters and the books that may be interpreted. The passage set

---

[47] *Shemot Rabbah* 8:2.

[48] *Bemidbar Rabbah* 14:4.

[49] Rivka Ulmer, "Theological Foundations of Rabbinic Hermeneutics." In: *Encyclopedia of Midrash*, vol. 2, 944–64.

forth below illustrates some of the major limits of *Midrash*: only certain books are subject to rabbinic interpretation and only a certain group (the Rabbis) that derives its authority from Sinai is permitted to interpret Scripture. Once the canon of the Hebrew Bible was closed, only the twenty-four books of Scripture could be interpreted, because these books were tossed "like a ball" from Sinai. Rarely do we find interpretations of extra-canonical books, such as *Ben Sira*, in the Midrashic corpus. God, "the shepherd," is the source of the messages and multiple interpretations contained in Scripture:

> "Another interpretation: *As nails* [*masmerot*] *well fastened* (Eccl. 12:11). From this the Sages have inferred that it is forbidden to read the non-canonical books; for it is written, *As nails* [*masmerot*] *well fastened*, which may be read *mishmarot*: as there are twenty-four priestly divisions [*mishmarot*] so there are also twenty-four books in Scripture. *Those that are composed in collections,* this applies to the Sanhedrin. Should you object that while one Sage permits, another prohibits; while one disqualifies, another declares fit; while one rules that a thing is unclean, another rules that it is clean; while Rabbi Eleᶜazar condemns, Rabbi Yehoshuᶜa acquits; while the House of Shammai disqualify, the House of Hillel declare fit; to whom then shall we listen? The Holy One, blessed be He, says: *They are all given from one shepherd* (ibid.)."[50]

Rabbinic hermeneutics is the mediator between the Written Torah and its companion, the Oral Torah, which is recreated in *Midrash*. Furthermore, Rabbinic hermeneutics and the hermeneutic rules applied by the Sages function as a mediator between the Torah and the agendas of the Rabbis. Generally, one may assume that a religious system would specify how humans can gain access to Divine revelation and would justify the reasons for staying within its parameters.[51] The creators of the *Midrashim* make explicit their exegetical reasoning by the application of hermeneutic rules. The rules

---

[50] *Bemidbar Rabbah* 15:22.

[51] Jacob Neusner, *From Literature to Theology in Formative Judaism: Three Preliminary Studies* (Atlanta: Scholars Press, 1989).

assisted in decoding the Bible, which contains the revealed word of God, which is somewhat different from the language that humans use for purposes of communication. The Oral and the Written Torah are separate but complementary.[52] The oral tradition is regained and projected into the future through the rabbinic hermeneutic rules and the ensuing norms and explanations that make the Torah relevant and, additionally, presents the theology of the interpreters.

Comparisons of rabbinic approaches to biblical interpretation to other cultures must take into consideration that in ancient Greece there had been interpreters of the sacral law. Furthermore, there are parallels between halakhic exegesis and the Greco-Roman system of legal interpretation[53] and Hellenistic rhetoric.[54] However, to ascertain the origin of certain hermeneutic rules is often impossible because of the nature of *Midrash*, which does not explain the source of the hermeneutic rules beyond an etiological legend. Nevertheless, rabbinic exegesis of the authoritative text, the Hebrew Bible, may be compared to a similar hermeneutic enterprise of the Alexandrian grammarians, who wrote exegetical comments on Homer, and Jewish Bible interpretation in Alexandria. Rabbinic exegesis as found in *Midrash* represents a unique initiative of the Rabbis of late antiquity since *Midrash* is a hermeneutic discourse *per se*.[55]

The Tannaitic tradition establishes three sets of rules of biblical interpretation: (1) the "Seven Rules of Hillel", (2) the "Thirteen Rules of Rabbi Yishmaᶜel", and (3) the "Thirty-two rules of Rabbi

---

[52] Irving Jacobs, *The Midrashic Process: Tradition and Interpretation in Rabbinic Judaism* (New York: Cambridge University Press, 1995).

[53] David Daube, "Alexandrian Methods of Interpretation and the Rabbis." In *Essays in Greco-Roman and Related Talmudic Literature* (ed. H. A. Fischel; New York: Ktav, 1977), 23–44.

[54] Philip Alexander, "Quid Athenis et Hierosolymis? Rabbinic Midrash and Hermeneutics in the Greco-Roman World." In: *A Tribute to Geza Vermes* (eds. P. R. White and R. T. Davies; Sheffield: Sheffield Academic Press, 1990), 101–24.

[55] Rivka Ulmer, "The advancement of arguments in exegetical *Midrash* compared to that of the Greek ΔΙΑΤΡΙΒΗ [*diatribe*]," *Journal for the Study of Judaism* 28,1 (1997), 48–91.

Eliʿezer." The thirteen rules (second century CE) are earlier than their cited Rabbis; the named Rabbis mainly collected and possibly amplified them. The thirty-two rules were only collected in the early medieval period, although they were applied earlier in Midrashic literature. The seven rules certainly existed before Hillel the Elder applied them (*Tosefta*, Sanhedrin 7:11); the time of their acceptance was probably the late first century BCE. The seven rules are stated in the introduction to *Sifra*: *A fortiori*, analogy, two verses, and a general statement and a particular statement, and something similar to it in another place, and a thing is explained from its context. Different schools of rabbinic study and teaching modified the rules in various ways. Rabbi ʿAkiva postulated that the divine language of the Torah is distinguished from human speech by the fact that in the former no word or sound is superfluous. Rabbi Yishmaʿel contended that the Torah speaks in human language (*Sifré Numbers* 112, p. 121; *Bereshit Rabbah* 1:14) and that there is no additional meaning attached to signs such as grammatical signs, doubling of words and adverbs in Scripture.

Rabbinic *Midrash* limits itself by its reliance upon the biblical text and the sets of hermeneutic rules that continued to expand. This definition would exclude any type of (post)modern *Midrash,* although the term *Midrash* has been applied to a variety of interpretative activities, from the use of biblical allusions in *Moby Dick* to interpretive dance and visual art.[56] In our view, *Midrash* was the rabbinic search for meaning in Scripture, and *Midrash* as a literary genre is limited to the rabbinic corpus of Midrashic works from late antiquity and the early Middle Ages. *Midrash* is primarily a text-based activity. The biblical text serves as a basis for the religious practice of the Rabbis; however, for the Rabbis the biblical text is rarely dependent upon any time reference in their exegetical enterprise. A biblical sign, like any other text, once it is separated from its source, produces a potentially infinite range of interpretations. Textual interpretation is inherent in the Hebrew Bible from the beginning, but the rabbinic interpreter understands Scripture's

---

[56] Marc Lee Raphael (ed.), *Agendas for the Study of Midrash in the Twenty-First Century* (Williamsburg, Va.: College of William and Mary, 1999).

meaning in his own time. Thus the present, at any given moment, creates the context of Scripture.

INTRODUCTION TO *TZEDAKAH* ("CHARITY") IN JUDAISM

During the course of Jewish history the term *Tzedakah* evolved in meaning. Initially during the biblical period the word was used in the sense of "righteousness." A *Tzadik*, such as Noah (Gen. 6:9), was a righteous individual. *Tzedakah* ("Charity") has been emphasized in Judaism since biblical times.[57] The *Torah* suggested that one tenth be collected for the poor (the poor person's tithe), and that corners of the field and the gleanings of the harvest be left for them so that they could participate in the harvest (*Pe'ah*). This was a way of providing for individuals who needed food and basic sustenance.[58] Many biblical passages continue this focus upon *Tzedakah*; those who neglected their poor fellow human beings were reprimanded.[59] Several classes of poor people, such as the widow, the orphan and the sick were mentioned, but no priorities were established.[60]

These ideas pertaining to *Tzedakah* were reinterpreted by the later Mishnaic, Midrashic and Talmudic literature. However, during the rabbinic period, approximately 200 CE until 600 CE, the same word, *Tzedakah,* had a new meaning. By that time, portions of the Jewish population lived in urban settings, so the earlier manner of distribution through gleanings and abandoned corners of the field were no longer appropriate. Although not universal in application, the primary use of *Tzedakah* during the above time period was in

---

[57] Franz Rosenthal, "Sedaka, Charity," *Hebrew Union College Annual* 23 (1950/51), 411–30. A bibliography is found in Rivka Ulmer, "Charity." In: *Reader's Guide to Judaism* (Chicago: Fitzroy Dearborn, 2000), 108–10.

[58] Lev. 19:27.30 ff.; Num. 18:26; Deut. 12:17; 2 Chr. 31:5 f.; Neh. 13:12.

[59] For example, Deut. 15:7 f.; Amos 2:6 ff.; Isa. 1:17; Jer. 7:6; Mal. 3:5; Prov. 30:10; Job 29:16.

[60] With regard to biblical sources, see Moshe Weinfeld, *Social Justice in Ancient Israel and in the Ancient Near East* (Jerusalem: Magnes Press, 1995), 33–9. Gary A. Anderson, *Charity: The Place of the Poor in the Biblical Tradition* (New Haven: Yale University Press, 2013).

the sense of "righteous giving." *Tzedakah* was deemed to be a *mitzvah*, a commandment, to assist others. Thus the English word "charity" is an inadequate translation of the rabbinic concept of *Tzedakah*. Charity implies that it is within the discretion of the donor as to whether to give, to whom and how much. From the rabbinic standpoint *Tzedakah* was a mandatory obligation upon every Jew and an elaborate system of restrictions, expectations and obligations were imposed upon both the donor and the donee (recipient). The *Mishnah* provided for the poor through the continuation of the tithes as well as the placement of gifts in a special area of the Temple from which individuals could help themselves according to their needs.

There are multiple regulations and discussions in the *Talmud* which deal with the poor and define those eligible for gifts. So, for example, those who still have enough provisions for two meals may participate in public food distribution in a soup kitchen, while those who still possess enough for twenty-four meals may not participate in distributions from a charitable box. Furthermore, those whose possessions consist of two *zuzim* could not glean in the fields.[61] Charity in the form of food or clothing was sometimes arranged by loans to the poor,[62] and every effort was made to adopt orphans and to arrange marriages for female orphans.[63] Even the poor are to be charitable.[64] There were additional rules about the sale of possessions and family responsibility for poor relatives.[65] The local poor were given priority over those at a distance, and members of the family over outsiders.[66] Gentiles could be beneficiaries of Jewish charity; the Jewish community took care of its own poor and except under special circumstances charity from

---

[61] *Mishnah,* Pe'ah 8.7–8; *Talmud Yerushalmi,* Pe'ah 29b.

[62] *Babylonian Talmud*, Yevamot 62b–63a.

[63] *Babylonian Talmud*, Sanhedrin 19b; Ketubbot 50a.

[64] *Babylonian Talmud*, Gittin 7b.

[65] *Babylonian Talmud*, Ketubbot 68a; see also *Shulḥan Arukh,* Yoreh Deah 253.1; 257.8.

[66] *Babylonian Talmud*, Bava Metzia 71a; *Mishnah*, Bava Kama 11:9; see also *Shulḥan Arukh*, Yoreh Deah 251.3.

Gentiles was not accepted.[67] Different forms of giving were mentioned and a few priorities concerning the distribution of *Tzedakah* were provided; the most preferable manner of distribution was the anonymous gift through which the donee (recipient) and the donor were unknown to each other. Charity is encouraged and required in multiple Talmudic and Midrashic passages.[68]

The objective of this book is to present the reader with an analysis of the above system of *Tzedakah* as created and understood by the rabbinic texts themselves. It is through these passages that we will have an opportunity to enter the rabbinic mind in order to comprehend their value system, their perceptions, their prospectives and their prejudices.

The discussion of *Tzedakah* will be limited to almsgiving and the giving of material goods, such as food and clothing. This book does not intend to explore the vast area of *Gemilut Ḥasadim* (acts of loving-kindness) that is found in rabbinic literature. There are some similarities between these two rabbinic expressions; however, we chose to limit the scope of this work to *Tzedakah*. *Tzedakah* for our purposes will be defined as the religious obligation of a donor to provide some portion of his/her material wealth to a donee. Passages in which *Tzedakah* was not utilized according to these definitions were rejected from consideration. Different passages in rabbinic literature were organized into different categories in order to provide a system of analysis. The passages were then translated into English with the objective of capturing some of the rabbinic parlance. The objective of the translations utilized in this book is to capture the essence of the language of the primary rabbinic sources to the greatest extent possible.

In regard to the biblical passages cited by the Rabbis, the primary translations came from the original and current translations published by The Jewish Publication Society of America. On some occasions, neither version was acceptable for the purposes of the

---

[67] *Mishnah*, Gittin 5:8; *Babylonian Talmud*, Gittin 61a–b; see also *Shulḥan Arukh,* Yoreh Deah 254.2.

[68] *Mishnah*, Avot 1:2; *Babylonian Talmud*, Bava Batra 9a–b, 109b; *Babylonian Talmud*, Berakhot 55a; *Babylonian Talmud*, Ketubbot 67b; *Babylonian Talmud*, Shabbat 156b; *Babylonian Talmud*, Taʿanit 20b.

particular text in question. In that case, our own version had to be utilized in order to capture the rabbinic understanding of the passage. On occasion, the textual analysis includes comments of speculation, since we can never be certain of the entire intellectual and emotional frame of reference of the authors of the texts.

Rabbinic literature is divided into aggadic and halakhic texts; the aggadic sections are mainly narrative, descriptive, and nonnormative texts that do not require a person to act, although the aggadic sections imply ethical standards of human behavior. The halakhic texts require a person to act in certain, normative ways. We do not distinguish between halakhic and aggadic texts in our presentation of different attitudes toward *Tzedakah*. Most textual examples relating to our topic are exegetical, utilizing biblical quotations to support rabbinic claims and arguments.

Since the rabbinic source material used in this book may be unfamiliar to many readers, the rabbinic texts are briefly described in the bibliography. For many of the rabbinic texts, dating cannot be precise and is sometimes given within the parameters of several centuries. Dating of rabbinic traditions is notoriously difficult, because unattributed, early traditions may appear in collections or works that were redacted much later than the rabbinic traditions and statements themselves. Even statements that are attributed to named authorities may be much earlier than these authorities. Rabbinic traditions chronologically belong to the Tannaitic period (70–220 CE), the Amoraic period (220–500 CE), or the post-Amoraic periods. Thus when we write about the rabbinic era or the rabbinic mind, we take into consideration that there are certain rabbinic conceptions that are in agreement with antecedent rabbinic views. This does not mean that all Rabbis over more than five centuries agreed on a particular point. Nevertheless, there is a certain conception of an idealistic Jewish culture that finds expression in a number of rabbinic texts;[69] *Tzedakah* is one of the concepts that

---

[69] On this point see Jay Harris, "From Inner-Biblical Interpretation to Early Rabbinic Exegesis." In: *Hebrew Bible, Old Testament: The History of Its Interpretation* (ed. Magne Sæbo; Göttingen, 1996), Vol. 1, 256–69, 256.

continually engaged the creators of rabbinic literature and Judaism until today.

CHAPTER ONE: THEOLOGY OF *TZEDAKAH*

"What did Adam say on the first day? *The earth is the Lord's and all that it holds, the world and its inhabitants* (Ps. 24:1).[1] To the rabbinic mind it was logical that Adam would quote the above verse. Adam's first perception of his environment required that he acknowledge God as the Creator of the universe and the Owner of all its contents. Thus from its inception, humanity was on notice that although it may temporarily retain possessions, ultimate ownership of all things belonged to God.

As Owner of the Land of Israel, God permitted certain members of Israelite society to temporarily possess the land. However, two distinctive castes were precluded from even such limited "ownership," namely the priestly class and the poor. What is the common link between the priests and the poor?

> "It is the common claim on God for protective support. Because neither group possesses a portion of the Land of Israel, neither can produce the food it needs. The priests, for their part, are forbidden by Scriptural law to own land (see Deut. 18:1–5). Instead, they act as God's servants in the Temple and are accorded food on that account. Similarly, the poor have lost whatever portion of the Land they may have possessed, and so are entitled to receive some of its yield. God supports both the priests and the poor because they neither own land

---

[1] *Avot de Rabbi Natan* 17, version b (Schechter edition); parallel in *Babylonian Talmud*, Rosh Hashanah 31a.

> nor attain the economic prosperity promised to all Israelites who live in the Land (see Deut. 8:7–10)."[2]

The above quotation is from an introduction to Tractate *Pe'ah*, which is a detailed rabbinic implementation of *Tzedakah* in respect to agriculture. In *Pe'ah* the claims upon God for protection of the priestly class and the poor are satisfied through the actions of the Israelite tenant farmer. The farmer is working on God's Land and consequently a portion of its yield belongs to God. The Israelite farmer has a dual obligation in respect to the produce: a portion must be tithed to the priests and another portion set aside for the benefit of the poor.

> "So underlying the designation of both priestly rations and poor-offerings is a single theory: God owns the entire Land of Israel and, because of this ownership, a portion of each crop must be paid to Him as a sort of sacred tax (see Lev. 27:30–33). According to Mishnah's framers, God claims that which is owed Him and then gives it to those under His special care, the poor and the priests."[3]

Thus one approach to understanding *Tzedakah* from a theological point of view is to deem *Tzedakah* "as a sort of sacred tax." This "sacred tax" is, in effect, an acknowledgment of God's benevolence. Furthermore, one has a responsibility in respect to the gifts that one has received from God. This concept is set forth in the following passage: *Honor the Lord with your substance* (Prov. 3:9). In explaining one's obligations pursuant to this verse, the Rabbis stated that it means:

> "From what He has bestowed upon you. He gave you a son — circumcise him; He gave you a house — make a *mezuzah* and build a parapet. He gave you a yard — build a *sukkah*; He gave

---

[2] Roger Brooks, *Support for the Poor in the Mishnaic Law of Agriculture: Tractate Peah* (Chico, CA: Scholars Press, 1983), 17–18. Gregg Elliot Gardner, *Giving to the Poor in Early Rabbinic Judaism* (PhD diss. Princeton, 2009).

[3] *Ibid.*, p. 18.

> you a flock — set aside the first born animal ... He gave you gold and silver — do *mitzvoth* with them ..."[4]

It is implied in the above passage that the *mitzvot* which one should perform in respect to one's "gold and silver" are to give *Tzedakah.* In addition, one has the obligation to distribute *Tzedakah* to the poor. This is due to God's special relationship with the poor. This unique relationship is three-fold in nature: 1) The poor are God's wards; 2) God is the champion of the poor; and 3) God, as a God of compassion, demands that those who are in a position to do so must help the less fortunate. As God's wards, the poor are members of one of His protected classes.

> "Rabbi Lulianus of Dromeah said in the name of Rabbi Yudah bar Simon that He [God] said [to Israel]: You have four classes of people in your household, your sons, your daughters, your male servants and your female servants. Similarly, I have four classes [in My household]: the Levites, the strangers, the orphans and the widows."[5]

The orphans and the widows are frequently mentioned by God, since they are the most visible poor, usually without the ability to sustain themselves. As members of a divinely protected class, the poor are entitled to divine legislation in which God commands others to assist the poor. The Rabbis commented upon this divine legislation in their analysis of the biblical verse in Prov. 22:22: *Do not rob the wretched because he is wretched; Do not crush the poor person in the gate.* The Rabbis asked:

> "What does Scripture refer to? If someone is poor, of what can s/he be robbed? Scripture therefore must refer to the gifts for the poor which one is obliged to give, the gleanings, the forgotten sheaves, the corners of the fields and the tithes. God warned that no person may rob them of these gifts which they are entitled to receive since they are poor. Not content with

---

[4] *Pesikta Rabbati* 25:4, Ulmer ed.

[5] *Pesikta de Rav Kahana* 11, 100a (Buber edition); see also Deut. 16:14.

> what the owner of the fields possesses, s/he would even rob the poor of that which God has granted them."[6]

In the Bible, God used the prophets to champion His cause for the poor. The prophetic championship left an indelible impression upon the rabbinic mind.

> "It has had the effect of inculcating in the mind of the Jew the realization that poverty is not a stigma of disgrace, nor a sign of inherent inferiority. Poverty might be due entirely to the existing standards of society, which permit injustice and greed to grow rampant."[7]

Thus one should not have contempt for the poor, rather they should be esteemed due to their closeness to God. Rabbinic literature emphasizes this close relationship. *Shemot Rabbah* states that the poor are God's nation.[8] *Babylonian Talmud*, Nedarim 81a, declares that "from among the poor goes forth the Torah."

God is compassionate as set forth in the Torah: *If you take your neighbor's garment in pledge, you must return it to him before the sun sets; it is his only clothing, the sole covering for his skin. In what else shall he sleep? If he cries out to Me, I will pay heed, for I am compassionate* (Exod. 22:25–27).

Since God is compassionate those human beings who lack compassion are defying God. To be devoid of a sense of compassion is, according to the Rabbis, a great sin. Concerning the rich men of Babylon, Rav said that they will go to *Gehinnom*, for when a scholar asked them for money to engage in business they refused. Consequently, these wealthy people must be descendants of the

---

[6] *Bemidbar Rabbah* 5:1.

[7] Mordecai M. Kaplan, "Jewish Philanthropy: Traditional and Modern." In: E. Farris, F. Laune, and A. Todd, (eds.), *Intelligent Philanthropy* (Chicago: University of Chicago Press, 1930), 52–89, 64. A survey and a discussion of the interrelationship of philanthropy and charity is found in Ephraim Frisch, *An Historical Survey of Jewish Philanthropy, From the Earliest Times to the Nineteenth Century* (New York: The MacMillan Company, 1924), 13ff.

[8] *Shemot Rabbah* 31:13.

mixed multitude that had accompanied the Israelites when they left Egypt.

> "For it is written: *And [He will] show you compassion and have compassion upon you* (Deut. 13:18). Thus, whoever is compassionate to his/her fellow human beings is certainly of the children of Abraham, and whosoever is not merciful to his/her fellow human beings is certainly not of the children of our father Abraham."[9]

The divine quality of compassion was instrumental in creating the universe. "With seven things the Holy One, blessed be He, created His world, namely: knowledge, understanding, might, loving-kindness and compassion, judgment and rebuke."[10] Since God created the people of Israel, compassion is also an essential element of their collective personality.

According to a rabbinic source, King David said:

> "This nation [Israel] is distinguished by three characteristics: [they are] compassionate, God-fearing and charitable. 'Compassionate,' for it is written, *And show you compassion, and in His compassion increase you as He promised your fathers on oath* (Deut. 13:18); 'God-fearing,' for it is written, *[Moses answered the people, Be not afraid, for God has come only in order to test you] and in order that the fear of Him may ever be with you, so that you do not go astray* (Exod. 20:20); 'Charitable,' for it is written: *For I have singled out Tzedakah and what is right, in order that the Lord may bring about for Abraham what He has promised him* (Gen. 18:19)."[11]

Consequently, it can be seen that being compassionate and giving *Tzedakah* are qualities that God expects from the people of Israel. God has this expectation since He demands that we imitate His divine attributes. This leads to *Imitatio Dei*, the imitation of God by humanity. By being compassionate, a human being likens himself/herself to his/her Creator. In analyzing a difficult word in the

---

[9] *Babylonian Talmud*, Betzah 32b.

[10] *The Fathers according to Rabbi Nathan* (transl. Judah Goldin; New York, 1955 [repr. 1974]), chapter 37, p. 153.

[11] *Babylonian Talmud*, Yevamot 79a.

verse: *The Lord is my strength and might; He has become my salvation. This is my God and I will enshrine Him, the God of my father and I will exalt Him* (Exod. 15:2), "Abba Shaul said: *I will enshrine Him* — that is to be like Him, just as He is gracious and compassionate, so you should be gracious and compassionate."[12]

There are two purposes as to why one should imitate the divine attributes of compassion in God. First is the *mitzvah* of the act itself which provides assistance to those in need. In addition, in performing an act of compassion one is ennobled and elevated. One sublimates the self through the action. "In a general sense these two aspects apply to all *mitsvot.* For aside from the purpose of the act of the *mitsvah qua* specific act of that particular *mitsvah* all *mitsvot* effect a refinement and sublimation of man … And conversely too, transgressions of the *mitsvot effect a spiritual defilement and obtuseness* …"[13] Thus for the rabbinic mind it was imperative that a human being, like God, should act with compassion.

> "How? Like the Holy One, may His great name be blessed forever and ever, He has compassion upon Israel wherever they dwell; His compassion is upon the poor and the needy, upon those who suffer and are in want, upon orphans when they require help and upon widows at all times. Similarly, a human being should be compassionate toward Israel wherever they dwell, compassionate toward the poor and the needy, toward those who suffer and are in want, toward orphans when they require help, and toward widows at all times, so that his own wife be not widowed and his own children be not orphaned, as it is said: *You shall not mistreat any widow or orphan. If you do mistreat them, I will heed their outcry as soon as they cry out to Me, and My anger shall blaze forth and I will put you to the sword, and your wives shall become widows and your children orphans* (Exod. 22:21–24)."[14]

---

[12] *Babylonian Talmud*, Shabbat 133b.

[13] Jacob I. Schochet, *Gemilut Chassadim* (Brooklyn, NY: Kehot Publications, 1967), 15.

[14] *Seder Eliyahu Rabah* 27, p. 143 (Friedmann edition).

God is the perfect role model for human beings. To the extent of their abilities human beings should duplicate the acts of God. God acts purposefully and His actions teach us how to behave. If we have questions about our moral conduct, we should look to God for guidance and inspiration. Rabbi Ḥama b. R. Ḥanina inquired as to the meaning of the verse *You shall walk after the Lord your God* (Deut. 13:5).

> "Is it possible for a person to walk after the *Shekhinah*? [This must mean] to walk after the attributes of the Holy One, blessed be He. Just as He clothes the naked, as it is written: *And the Lord God made for Adam and for his wife coats of skin, and clothed them* (Gen. 3:21), so you, too, should clothe the naked. The Holy One, blessed be He, visited the sick, as it is written: *And the Lord appeared unto him in the oaks of Mamre* (Gen. 18:1), so you, too, should visit the sick. The Holy One, blessed be He, buried the dead, as it is written: *And he buried him in the valley* (Deut. 34:6), so you, too, should bury the dead."[15]

It is interesting to note that according to the Rabbis, *Tzedakah* was not only practiced on earth; the angels themselves gave *Tzedakah*.

> "R. Ammi asked Rabbi Shmuʾel b. Naḥman, What is the meaning of the text: *Your Tzedakah also, O God, which reaches unto high heaven* … (Ps. 71:19)? He answered him, Just as the lower ones [human beings] need each other's *Tzedakah*, so do the upper ones [angels] need each other's *Tzedakah*. Thus it is written: *He spoke to the person clothed in linen* … (Ezek. 10:2)."[16]

The person clothed in linen in the above verse was a cherub; thus the cherubim wore clothes and some of them must have needed clothing, and thus the poorer ones, like humans, were in need of *Tzedakah*.

Not only did the angels perform *Tzedakah*, but God Himself did as well. The following passage compares various acts of *Tzedakah* by God and asks which is the greatest act of *Tzedakah*. In the first paragraph of the cited text, the idolatrous conduct of the

[15] *Babylonian Talmud*, Sotah 14a.

[16] *Vayikrah Rabbah* 31:1.

Danites is discussed. Nevertheless, God granted the Danites (the people of the tribe of Dan) victory in their war against the people of Laish. In the second paragraph, R. Shmuʾel bar Naḥmani declares that still a greater act of *Tzedakah* by God was His sending manna to the Hebrews even though they were still worshipping idols.

> "*They* [the Danites] *took that which Micah had made* (Judg. 18:27) — that is, the idol's image, *and the priest whom he had* (*ibid.*) — that is the idolatrous priest, *and they came unto Laish, unto a people quiet and secure* (*ibid.*) — they worshipped an idol and the idol brought them success. Is there any greater *Tzedakah*? *Unto You, O Lord, belongs Tzedakah, but unto us we have shame* (Dan. 9:7).
>
> R. Shmuʾel b. Naḥmani said: You find that the day that manna came down for Israel is the same day on which they worshipped idols. Even more, they took the manna and sacrificed it to their idols. That is what is written: *My bread also which I gave you* … (Ezek. 16:19)."[17]

Another theological explanation of *Tzedakah* is that God is constantly testing people to see how they respond to the needs of the poor. Thus one's moral character is revealed to God by how one reacts to the daily opportunities of performing *Tzedakah*. "Happy is the person who can withstand the test, for there is none whom God does not test. He tests the rich person to see if his/her hand is open to the poor …"[18]

Since the poor are a protected class of God, He is always near them and observes how they are treated. "R. Abun said: The poor person stands at your door, and the Holy One, blessed be He, stands at his/her right hand. If you give unto him/her, He who stands at his/her right hand will bless you, but if not, He will condemn you, as it is written, *Because He stands at the right hand of the needy, to save him from those who would condemn him* (Ps. 109:31."[19] Thus

---

[17] *Pesikta de Rav Kahana* 11, 99a (Buber edition).

[18] *Shemot Rabbah* 31:3.

[19] *Rut Rabbah* 5:9.

God is in an ideal position to administer the tests of whether or not one performs *Tzedakah* and to grade the examinee accordingly.

The uncertainty and unpredictability of life influenced the rabbinic mind set. A person could never be completely confident that he or she would retain their wealth. One could not afford to ignore the duty of giving *Tzedakah*, since one would never know when God would decide that the individual would himself/herself be in need.

> "Because there is an ever rotating wheel in this world, and s/he who is rich today may not be so tomorrow, and also s/he who is poor today may not be so tomorrow. One He casts down, and the other He raises up, as it says: *For God it is who gives judgment; He brings down one person, He lifts up another* (Ps. 75:8)."[20]

This uncertainty, which is expressed in the rabbinic texts, required one to avail oneself of every opportunity to give *Tzedakah*, since one could not be sure of the outcome of any particular act of *Tzedakah*.

> "R. Yehoshuʿa said: If you gave a *perutah* to a poor person in the morning and another poor person came and stood before you in the evening, give to her/him too; for you don't know if both acts from your hand will survive. As it is said: *Sow your seed in the morning, and don't hold back your hand in the evening, since you don't know which is going to succeed, the one or the other, or if both are equally good* (Eccl. 11:6)."[21]

In addition to the uncertainty in their world, the Rabbis were concerned with theodicy as well. In particular, they asked themselves why this evil known as poverty existed.[22] Why did God permit people to be poor? A rabbinic response to this troubling question is found in the following passage concerning a dialogue between a skeptical Gentile, Turnus Rufus, and Rabbi ʿAkiva.

---

[20] *Shemot Rabbah* 31:3.

[21] *Avot de Rabbi Natan* 3, version a (Schechter edition).

[22] Ford J. Massyngberde, "Three ancient Jewish views of poverty." In: *New Way of Jesus* (Newton, Kan: Faith and Life Press, 1980), 39–55.

> "And this question was asked by Turnus Rufus to R. ʿAkiva: If your God loves the poor why does He not support them? He said: So that we may be saved through them from the punishment of *Gehinnom.* I will tell you a simile. What is this thing like? To a king of flesh and blood who was angry with his servant and put him in prison and ordered concerning him that he should not be given food or drink. And a servant went and gave him food and drink. When the king heard this, would he not be angry with him? And you are called servants, as it is written: *For it is to Me that the Israelites are servants; they are My servants whom I freed from the land of Egypt, I the Lord their God* (Lev. 25:55).
>
> R. ʿAkiva responded: I will tell you a simile, What is this thing like? To a king of flesh and blood who was angry with his son and put him in a prison and ordered concerning him that he should not be given food or drink. A man went and gave him food and drink. When the king heard this, would he not send him a present? And we are called sons, as it is written: *You are the sons of the Lord your God* (Deut. 14:1).
>
> Turnus Rufus said to him: You are called both sons and servants. When you do according to the will of God you are called sons and when you do not according to the will of God, you are called servants. And now you are not doing according to the will of God.
>
> R. ʿAkiva replied: *It is not to share your bread with the hungry and to take the wretched poor into your home? When you see the naked, to clothe them and not to ignore your own kin* (Isa. 58:7)."[23]

In the first portion of the above passage, Rabbi ʿAkiva is confronted with the perplexing problem of how a compassionate God could allow so much suffering by the poor. Why did He create the poor? Rabbi ʿAkiva's response indicates that to the rabbinic mind,

---

[23] *Babylonian Talmud*, Bava Batra 10a.

the poor were an instrumentality for salvation.[24] By assisting the poor, by giving them *Tzedakah*, one may avoid the punishment of *Gehinnom*. The concept of reward and punishment in respect to *Tzedakah* will be discussed in subsequent chapters of this book.

After the initial explanation by R. ᶜAkiva, the skeptic Turnus Rufus contends that since God created the poor this must be His desire. Since He has His reasons, any efforts to ameliorate the condition of the poor would be deemed by God as an act of disobedience by His "servants." In rebuttal, R. ᶜAkiva submits that another analogy is more appropriate. Since the poor, as well as the rest of humanity, are all "sons" of God, then God would certainly be grateful if some of the children of God helped His poor "son." In response, Turnus Rufus states that the Israelites are known by two different designations, as "servants" and as "sons." When they are disobedient they are "servants" and when they are obedient they are "sons." By performing *Tzedakah* they must be disobedient "servants." In the final repartee of the argument, R. ᶜAkiva abandons the servant-son distinction and simply quotes the above passage of Isa. 58:7 which requires of all humanity that they respond to the needs of the poor.

It should also be kept in mind that the Rabbis were quite aware of their mission to perform *Tikun ᶜOlam*, repair of the world.[25] They believed that the world was not perfect and that God created humanity to effectuate positive change on this planet. Helping the poor, performing *Tzedakah*, would certainly be consistent with this divine purpose of humanity. In a dialogue similar to the above, a philosopher was asking the same kind of question to R. Oshaᶜyah. The rabbinic response was: "All that was created during the six days of creation requires improvement. For example, the mustard and the lupine seed need sweetening, the wheat needs to be ground, and even a person needs improvement."[26]

---

[24] Alyssa M. Gray, "Redemptive Almsgiving and the Rabbis of Late Antiquity," *Jewish Studies Quarterly* 18 (2011), 144–84, 161, focuses on the salvific character of almsgiving for the individual.

[25] *The Dynamics of Tzedakah* (Jerusalem: The Shalom Hartmann Institute for Advanced Judaic Studies, 1981).

[26] *Bereshit Rabbah* 11:6.

Thus it can be seen that the performance of *Tzedakah* is partially fulfilling God's mission for humanity and thus would bring us closer to God. This line of reasoning is evident in the following rabbinic passage:

> "R. Le'azar b. R. Yose said: From where [in Scripture can we learn that] *Tzedakah* and *Gemilut Ḥasadim* [cause] great peace and are a great link between Israel and their Father in Heaven, as it says, *For thus says the Lord: Enter not into the house of mourning, neither go to lament, neither bemoan them; for I have taken away My peace from this people, says the Lord, even loving-kindness and compassion* (Jer. 16:5). 'Loving-kindness' is *Gemilut Ḥasadim* and 'compassion' is *Tzedakah* which teaches us that *Tzedakah* and *Gemilut Ḥasadim* cause a great peace between Israel and their Father in Heaven."[27]

The above passage alludes to the strong connection between *Tzedakah* and peace. By performing *Tzedakah* we enhance the prospects of peace in this world. Under the divine scheme, *Tzedakah* and peace are interrelated and interdependent. Thus we have the famous phrase: "The more *Tzedakah* the more peace."[28]

---

[27] *Tosefta*, Pe'ah 4:21, p. 61 (Lieberman edition); parallel in *Babylonian Talmud*, Bava Batra 10a.

[28] *Mishnah*, Avot 2:7.

CHAPTER TWO: THE RABBINIC VIEW OF POVERTY AND THE HUMILIATION OF ACCEPTING *TZEDAKAH*

One's obligation in respect to *Tzedakah* depended to some extent upon the particular circumstances of the donor. One's responsibilities were not limited to the assistance of only those members of society who spent their entire lifespan on the lowest economic rung. A formerly wealthy individual who was without meat and wine could be an appropriate recipient of *Tzedakah*. Preserving and enhancing the dignity of the individual recipient was of paramount concern to the Rabbis. Consequently, "poverty" should be understood as a relative term in rabbinic literature. Since the individual was to satisfy the particular needs of each individual, what may be deemed as "wealth" for one person may be concurrently considered "poverty" by another. Thus, the reader should keep in mind this rather "flexible" understanding of the condition of poverty. Nevertheless, the Rabbis struggled to define poverty. One attempt is found in the following text:

> "Eight names were given to the poor man: *ʿani*, *evyon*, *misken*, *rash*, *dal*, *dakh*, *makh*, and *helekh*, *ʿAni* means 'poor' in its literal sense; *evyon* because s/he longs [*meta'ev*] for everything; *misken* because s/he is despised by all, as it says, *Wisdom is better than strength, nevertheless the poor man's wisdom is despised, and his words are not heard* (Eccl. 9:16); *rash* because s/he is dispossessed [*mitroshesh*] of property; *dal* because s/he is detached [*meduldal*] from property; *dakh* because s/he is crushed [*medukhdakh*] — s/he sees a thing and cannot eat it, s/he sees a thing and cannot drink it; *makh* because s/he is lowly [*makh*] before everyone, like a kind of lowly threshold. Accordingly, Moses warns Israel: *If your brother is very poor,* [*and sells some of his possessions, then shall*

> *his kinsman that is next to him come, and shall redeem that which his brother has sold*] (Lev. 25:25)."[1]

Even using some of the concepts listed above, one should readily see that it could apply to various people depending upon their previous station in life. A formerly rich individual may be crushed (*medukhdakh*) because s/he cannot eat expensive meat and drink costly wine any longer. A person who has been destitute all her/his life may be crushed that s/he has absolutely nothing edible to put into her/his stomach.

The predominant rabbinic view was that poverty was a permanent condition that would always be endured by at least some members of society. Even in the messianic era poverty would continue. "For Shmuʾel said: There is no difference between this world and the days of the Messiah except for oppression through foreign powers, as it says: *For the poor shall never cease out of the land* … (Deut. 15:11)."[2] Since poverty will always be with us, each one of us has the responsibility to alleviate the evil and suffering of poverty. This is one of our major roles in our mission to perform *Tikkun ʿOlam* (See chapter one).

Since poverty would exist in each generation, one could not safely assume that poverty would never touch one's family or one's descendants. To the contrary, since humanity cannot totally escape from poverty, sooner or later it will visit its misfortune upon every family.

> "It was taught, R. Eleʿazar Ha-Kappar said: A person should always pray for mercy to be spared this fate [poverty], for if s/he does not come into poverty her/his son will, and if not her/his son, her/his grandson, for it is said, *because that for* [*bigelal*] *this thing* … (Deut. 15:10). The School of Rabbi Yishmaʾel taught: It is a wheel [*galgal*] that revolves in the world."[3]

---

[1] *Vayikra Rabbah* 34:6.

[2] *Babylonian Talmud*, Berakhot 34b.

[3] *Babylonian Talmud*, Shabbat 151b; parallel *Rut Rabbah* 5:9.

To understand the above fatalistic philosophy that to some extent poverty is beyond one's control, we need to examine the following two verses: *Beware that there be not a base thought in your heart, saying: The seventh year, the year of release, is at hand; and your eye be evil against your needy brother, and you give him nothing; and he cry unto the Lord against you, and it be sin in you. You shall surely give him and your heart shall not be grieved when you give unto him; because [bigelal] that for this thing the Lord your God will bless you in all your work, and in all that you put your hand unto* (Deut. 15:9–10). The key word in the text is "because" since in Hebrew the word for "because" [*bigelal*] contains the letters for "wheel" [*galgal*]. From this text the Rabbis contended that a realistic perspective of poverty is that it is similar to a revolving wheel that will eventually touch every family. (See chapter one in reference to the uncertainty and unpredictability of life).

This wheel of poverty is driven by God's will and is not within the control of humanity. In commenting upon the phrase *even to the poor with you* which is found in the following verse, *if you lend money to any of My people, even to the poor with you, you shall not be to him as a creditor; neither shall you lay upon him interest* (Exod. 22:24). The Rabbis quoted another critical verse *For God is judge; He puts down one and lifts up another* (Ps. 75:8) and offered the following explanation:

> "To what is the world likened? To a wheel in a garden; the earthenware vessels attached to it ascend full from below and descend empty from above. In the same way the one who is not rich today is rich tomorrow, and s/he who is poor today is not poor tomorrow. Why? Because there is a rotating wheel in the world, as it is written, *Because [bigelal] that for this thing …* (Deut. 15:10). Rabbi Aḥa said, There is a wheel that rotates in this world, because it says, *A wise king sifts the wicked, and turns the wheel [ofan] over them* (Prov. 20:26)."[4]

In this text an alternative word for wheel, *ofan*, is used as well as *galgal* from the word *bigelal*. The concept of the cyclical nature of life remains unchanged. The metaphor of a rotating wheel is found frequently in rabbinic literature. In juxtaposition to the words *You shall surely give him* (Deut. 15:10) cited by Rabbi Aivo, "R. Naḥman

---

[4] *Shemot Rabbah* 31:14.

said: *Because* [*bigelal*] *that for this thing* (*ibid.*), *bigelal* means that this world is like a pumping-wheel [*galgela*] through which the full is emptied and the empty is filled."[5] In this case the "full" are the rich and the "empty" are the poor.

Another analogy utilized by the Rabbis to demonstrate the ever-changing nature of wealth and poverty is that of ladders given by God to humans that cause their ascent or descent on the rungs of economic fortune.

> "A *matrona* [Roman lady] asked R. Yose b. Ḥalafta. She said to him: Everybody admits that in six days God created the world. From those six days until now, what has He been doing? He said to her: He causes people to ascend ladders of fortune and to descend ladders, saying, So-and-so who was rich shall become poor, and so-and-so who was poor shall become rich, as it is stated, *The Lord makes poor, and makes rich* … (1 Sam. 2:7)."[6]

A similar *Midrash* makes the same point but cites a different scriptural verse:

> "A *matrona* [Roman lady] asked R. Shimᶜon b. Ḥalafta: In how many days did the Holy One, blessed be He, create the world? He said to her: In six, as it says, *For in six days the Lord made heaven and earth* (Exod. 20:11). She said: What has He been doing from then until now? He said: He sits and makes ladders, whereby He elevates one and puts down another. Accordingly it says, *For God is judge; He puts down one, and lifts up another* (Ps. 75:8)."[7]

The Rabbis were quite aware that wealth and poverty were ephemeral phenomena that were constantly in flux. They used puns to illustrate this perception. "Therefore, wealth is called *nekhasim* because it is concealed [*nekhsin*] from one and revealed to another. Why are certain coins called *zuzin*? Because they are removed [*zazin*] from one and given to another."[8]

---

[5] *Vayikra Rabbah* 34:9.

[6] *Bemidbar Rabbah* 3:6.

[7] *Bemidbar Rabbah* 22:8; parallel *Bereshit Rabbah* 68:4.

[8] *Bemidbar Rabbah* 22:8.

The economic destiny of every human being was in the hands of God. God ultimately decided whether one would be rich or poor and the duration of such status. In commenting upon the verse *The rich and poor meet together — The Lord is the Maker of them all* (Prov. 22:2), the Rabbis stated that God made "the poor person who stretches out his/her hand, and the householder who does not want to give him/her anything; He who made this one rich will in the future make him poor, and He who made this one poor will in the future make him rich."[9]

Immediately following the above passage attributing to God the role of fashioning everyone's financial circumstances, the editor continues with his assessment of the condition of poverty. "Nothing is harder to bear than poverty; for s/he who is crushed by poverty is like one to whom all the sufferings of the world cling and upon whom all the curses in Deuteronomy came. Our teachers said: If all suffering were assembled on one side and poverty on the other, poverty would outweigh them."[10]

Over and over again in rabbinic texts a reader will find that the rabbinic view of poverty was that it was a terrible evil; perhaps the worst suffering that a human could endure.

> "R. Pinḥas b. Ḥama gave this exposition: Poverty in one's house is worse than fifty plagues, for it is said, *Have pity upon me, have pity upon me, O you my friends; for the hand of God has touched me* (Job 19:21), and his friends answered him, *Take heed, regard not iniquity; for this have you chosen rather than poverty* (Job 16:21)."[11]

The above rabbinical interpretation depends upon mathematical extrapolation. Since ten plagues were inflicted upon the Egyptians before the Exodus from Egypt with one finger of God (Exod. 8:15), then fifty plagues must have been inflicted upon Job since he was touched by the hand of God, which, like a human hand, has five fingers. In any event, the above quote is useful in depicting the rabbinic hyperbole that matched poverty against virtually all other

---

[9] *Shemot Rabbah* 31:14.

[10] *Shemot Rabbah* 31:14; see also *Shemot Rabbah* 31:12.

[11] *Babylonian Talmud*, Bava Batra 116a.

sufferings. Poverty was considered to be the most difficult to endure. In fact, poverty undermined the very foundation of life and reduced one to the status of a dead person. Four categories of individuals are accounted for as dead. One of these categories is that of a poor person.[12]

What was the reason that poverty was characterized by the Rabbis as such an unbearable agony? The explanation is that poverty reduced one to economic dependence upon others. This dependence had the potential of destroying one's dignity and self-esteem. What could be worse than this?

Once one became dependent upon others for survival, a radical change devastated the individual and took its toll.

> "And R. Natan b. Abba said in the name of Rav: Someone who is dependent on another's table, the world is dark to him/her, for it is said: *He wanders abroad for bread: Where is it? He knows that the day of darkness is ready at his hand* (Job 15:23). R. Ḥisda says: Also his life is no life. Our Rabbis taught: There are three whose life is no life and they are: S/he who is dependent on the table of his neighbor ..."[13]

A person becomes quickly affected by his/her dependency. "When a person eats of his/her own food his/her heart is gratified, but when s/he eats from the food of others his/her heart is embittered."[14]

Thus, poverty leads to the humiliation of being dependent upon *Tzedakah* for one's own survival. This humiliation negatively transforms one in both a physical and spiritual sense.

> "R. Yoḥanan and R. Eliʿezer both say: As soon as a human being needs the support of his/her fellow-creatures his/her face is like the *kerum*, as it is said: *As the kerum is to be reviled among the sons of men* (Ps. 12:9). What is the *kerum*? When R. Dimi came he said: There is a bird in the coastal towns whose name is *kerum*, and as soon as the sun shines upon it, it changes into

---

[12] *Babylonian Talmud*, Nedarim 64b.

[13] *Babylonian Talmud*, Betsah 32b.

[14] *Seder Eliyahu Rabah* 25, p. 136 (Friedmann edition).

> several colors. R. Ammi and R. Asi both say: [When a person needs the support of his/her fellow-beings] it is as if s/he were punished with two punishments, with fire and water. For it is said: *When You have caused people to ride over our heads, we went through fire and through water* (Ps. 66:12)."[15]

In the above passage the Rabbis are making a pun on the word *kerum* which in the biblical verse cited (Ps. 12:9) is understood as "vileness." However, there was a bird also with the name of *kerum* which perhaps as part of its camouflage readily changed colors. Similarly, the human recipient of *Tzedakah* changed colors, commenced to blush, due to his/her immense sense of humiliation.

The recipient of *Tzedakah* accepts a "gift" from the donor; however, this "gift" is not entirely free. The donee inevitably pays a price, usually a loss of independence and perhaps a loss of self-worth. The Rabbis did not look favorably upon receiving these types of "gifts." "When receivers of gifts multiplied, the days of human life became fewer and years were shortened; as it is written, *But he that hates gifts shall live* (Prov. 15:27)."[16]

Consequently, due to the rabbinic perception of poverty and its fostering of dependence, one should pray that one not be reduced to relying upon "gifts" of another. It was permissible to rely upon God, but it was onerous to rely upon other human beings for sustenance. One such prayer is found in the following beautiful *Midrash* that inquires as to why the dove in the Noah story returned with an olive branch in its beak.

> "R. Yirmeah b. Eleʿazar said: What is it that is written, *And lo in her mouth an olive-leaf freshly plucked* (Gen. 8:11)? The dove said to the Holy One, blessed be He, Master of the universe, may my food be as bitter as the olive but entrusted to Your hand rather than sweet as honey and dependent on a mortal …"[17]

---

15 *Babylonian Talmud*, Berakhot 6b.

16 *Babylonian Talmud*, Sotah 47b.

17 *Babylonian Talmud*, ʿEruvin 18b.

This dread of being compelled to accept *Tzedakah* led the Rabbis to encourage others to do everything in their power to prevent this tragedy. A great tragedy would occur if one's children had to rely upon *Tzedakah*. As a parent, the father did not have to support his children for the balance of their lives. However, if the children were reduced to a desperate situation in which they would become dependent upon *Tzedakah*, the Rabbis often made an exception in regard to parental responsibility.

> "When a man came before Rava he said to him: Will it please you that your children should be fed from *Tzedakah*? This ruling, however, has been laid down only for one who is not a wealthy person, but if the person is wealthy s/he may be forced even against his/her will, as was the case with Rava who used compulsion against R. Natan b. Ammi and extracted from him four hundred *zuz* for *Tzedakah*."[18]

In this passage it is first acknowledged that a father cannot be compelled to support his children under certain circumstances. However, the above ruling was only limited to a person who himself/herself was not wealthy. Since Rava was able to extract *Tzedakah* from a reluctant but wealthy individual, how much more so should one be able to compel a wealthy father to support his own children, even beyond their maturity, if the alternative was their dependence upon *Tzedakah*.

This same viewpoint is found in another text which urges the family to exhaust its funds before it permits the children to be supported by *Tzedakah*. "Rabban Shimᶜon b. Gamliel says that Rabbi Meir used to say: If somebody says, give a *shekel* from my sons on *Shabbat*, and if they are worthy to take a *selaʾ*, they give them a *selaʾ* and for the rest they are supported from *Tzedakah*. The wise say, they are fed and go until the money is used up and [only] then are they supported by *Tzedakah*."[19]

Given the above point of view about the humiliation of accepting *Tzedakah*, the Rabbis urged the people to accept virtually any type of honest work rather than being dependent upon others.

---

18 *Babylonian Talmud*, Ketubbot 49b.

19 *Tosefta*, Ketubbot 6:10.

Work was honorable in itself and one should not disdain manual labor or the unpleasant tasks inherent in such work. This "work ethic" is described in the following text.

> "I have received [the following tradition] from my grandfather's family: At all times shall one rather hire oneself out to idol-worship than be in need of one's fellow creatures. He meant actual *ʿAvodah Zarah*[20] [idolatry], but it is not so, *ʿAvodah Zarah* is work which is strange to him, as Rav said to R. Kahana: Flay a carcass in the street and earn a wage, and say not, I am a great man and the work is degrading to me."[21]

In the rabbinic world under the Romans,[22] work was inherently valuable to one's self-esteem and had a definite place in everyone's life. One of the most sacred human activities for the Rabbis was the study of Torah. However, even Torah study should not justify a total rejection of work. "All study of the Law without toil must in the end prove futile and lead to sin."[23]

Although work was highly valued by the Rabbis it could be the height of insensitivity to remind a supplicant for *Tzedakah* of this. One could never be sure of the circumstances of the individual who was seeking *Tzedakah.* God would punish those who are cruelly insensitive to the applicant for *Tzedakah.*

> "If the rich person says to this same poor person: Why do you not go and work and get food? Look at those hips! Look at those legs! Look at that belly! Look at those lumps of flesh! The Holy One, blessed be He, says to him: It is not enough that you have not given him anything of yours, but you set an evil eye upon what I have given him. Consequently, *If he has produced a son, there is nothing in his hand* (Eccl. 5:13). He produces a son and he will not leave anything at all of his possessions,

---

[20] Literally: "strange worship."

[21] *Babylonian Talmud*, Bava Batra 110a; parallel *Babylonian Talmud*, Pesaḥim 113a.

[22] Lee I. Levine, *The Rabbinic Class of Roman Palestine in Late Antiquity* (Jerusalem: Yad Yitzḥak Ben-Zvi Publications, 1989), pp. 69–72.

[23] *Mishnah*, Avot 2:2.

> nor take unto himself anything. Accordingly Moses warns Israel: *If your brother is very poor, and sells some of his possessions, then shall his kinsman that is next to him come, and shall redeem that which his brother has sold* (Lev. 25:25)."[24]

Although work was highly valued, one could not exacerbate the plight of the victim by reminding him/her of this value while s/he was attempting to collect *Tzedakah*. One could not turn away from one's responsibilities.[25] One had to positively respond in some fashion when confronted with the obligation of giving *Tzedakah*. Turning away from this responsibility was considered a great sin.

> "Whoever turns away her/his eyes from *Tzedakah* is considered as if s/he were serving idols. It is written here, *Beware that there be not a base thought in your heart* (Deut. 15:9) and it is written there, *Certain base fellows are gone out* (Deut. 13:14). Just as there is idolatry, also here is idolatry."[26]

In the first passage above it was a base thought and a sin to give one's needy fellow human being nothing (Deut. 15:9). In the second passage (Deut. 13:14) the same word for "base" is utilized. The verse reads: *Certain base fellows are gone out from your midst, and have drawn away the inhabitants of their city, saying: Let us go and serve other gods, which you have not known.* In the first instance it was "base" not to give *Tzedakah* to the needy and in the second instance it was "base" to encourage others to commit idolatry. For the rabbinic mind both sets were comparable and equally egregious.

From the rabbinic perspective, the failure to give *Tzedakah*, the failure to positively respond to the needs of another human being was a great sin. One should value other people's dignity to be as precious as one's own. Rabbi ᶜAkiva stated that the major principle of the Torah is found in the verse, *You shall love your neighbor as*

---

[24] *Vayikra Rabbah* 34:4; parallel *Vayikra Rabbah* 34:7, *Kohelet Rabbah* 5:12, 1.

[25] Joseph Feinstein, *Am I My Brother's Keeper* (New York: Jewish Education Committee Press, 1970), 21, presents this argument in the context of societal responsibilities beyond Judaism.

[26] *Babylonian Talmud*, Bava Batra 10a.

yourself (Lev. 19:18). In commenting upon the above position of Rabbi ʿAkiva it has been written: "No one should say, Just as I have been humiliated, so, also, let others be humiliated. R. Tanḥuma said: If you do so, know whom you are humiliating: *You are made in the likeness of God* (Gen. 5:1)."[27]

[27] *Bereshit Rabbah* 24:7.

CHAPTER THREE: THE REWARDS OF GIVING *TZEDAKAH*

A vast amount of rabbinic literature exists pertaining to the topic of the rewards of giving *Tzedakah*. Consequently, in order to facilitate analysis the subject matter has been divided into six separate subcategories. These subdivisions are as follows: A) eligibility to obtain the reward; B) the power of *Tzedakah*; C) reciprocity of benefit between the donor and the donee; D) benefits obtained during one's lifetime; E) the miracle stories; F) benefits in the World to Come.

ELIGIBILITY TO OBTAIN THE REWARD

Merely because one gives *Tzedakah* does not automatically entitle one to be rewarded. From the perspective of the Rabbis there were certain eligibility requirements. First, the Rabbis did not endorse the "Robin Hood" mentality; stealing from the rich and giving to the poor did not entitle one to any benefits. In interpreting the following verse: *Better is a handful of quietness than both hands full of labor* (Eccl. 4:6), the Rabbis explained that the phrase *better a handful of quietness* means "better is he who practices *Tzedakah* to a small extent from his own [assets] than one who steals, robs and oppresses and gives much *Tzedakah* from what belongs to others. A proverb states: She prostitutes herself for apples and gives them to the sick."[1]

Furthermore, one cannot knowingly engage in sin and then expect the sin instantly purged by an act of *Tzedakah*. Such a practice would undermine the concept of *Teshuvah*. Giving *Tzedakah* does not result in divine permission to commit sin.

[1] *Kohelet Rabbah* 4:1,6.

"R. Yoḥanan said: A simile about a man who committed a sin, and he had given a payment to a prostitute and had not yet left her doorstep when a poor person approached him. The poor individual said: Give me alms [*Tzedakah*]. He gave him alms and he walked away. The same man said: If the Holy One, blessed be He, had not wanted to forgive my sins, He would not have sent this poor man [to me] in order that I give him alms [*Tzedakah*] and thus be forgiven for what I did. The Holy One, blessed be He, spoke to him: Wicked man, do not think so. But go and learn from the wisdom of Solomon: The hand which gives will not cleanse the other from the evil."[2]

There is another limitation upon the eligibility to obtain rewards from giving *Tzedakah.* (This issue will be discussed in chapter seventeen.)

In addition to the above restrictions, the quality of the reward is dependent upon how the act of *Tzedakah* was performed. For example, if *Tzedakah* is given discreetly the reward would be much greater than if *Tzedakah* was given indiscreetly. The grace, the gentleness, the compassion and empathy that accompany the act of *Tzedakah* affect the rewards. R. Eleᶜazar[3] summarized this position by stating: "The reward of *Tzedakah* is dependent upon the amount of *Ḥesed* [loving-kindness] in it, for it is written: *sow yourselves according to Tzedakah, reap according to Ḥesed* (Hos. 10:12)."[4]

The above theme is further illustrated by the following quotation: "Now, my children, have pity and compassion on all men, that the Lord may have pity and compassion on you, for in the measure in which a person has mercy with his/her fellow human beings, God has mercy with him/her."[5] Furthermore, the poor and the *Tzedakah* they are given enable the rich to attain merit.

"R. Tanḥum b. R. Ḥiyya would do the following: When his mother would fetch for him a measure of meat from the mar-

---

[2] See Prov. 11:21. *Midrash Mishle* 11, p. 35a, Buber edition.

[3] In regard to Rabbi Eleᶜazar, see Eliezer Lorne Segal, "Rabbi Eleazar's 'perutah'," *Journal of Religion* 85 (2005), 25–42.

[4] *Babylonian Talmud*, Sukkah 49b.

[5] In the Pseudepigrapha, in *Testament of Zebulun* 1–8.

ket, she would get two [measures], one for him and one for the poor. When she would get a measure of vegetables from the market, [she would get] one for him and one for the poor, as it is written: *The one no less than the other was God's doing* (Eccl. 7:14). Rich and poor, so that these might give alms to those [the poor], and those [the poor] might make worthy these [the rich]."[6]

Like in the story of Abba Yudan (see p. 78), the poor play a supporting role in this story; they enable the rich to gain merit or the "gift of recompense."

THE POWER OF *TZEDAKAH*

As explained in chapter one, the practice of *Tzedakah* establishes a strong link between humanity and God. In fact, the giving of *Tzedakah* brings humans and God into close contact. For example, the Rabbis commented upon the scriptural verse: *With Tzedek I shall see your face* (Ps. 17:15). This verse does not actually use the word *Tzedakah*. Nevertheless, the Rabbis construed this passage to refer to the practice of *Tzedakah*. "Come and see how great the power of *Tzedakah* is. For one *perutah* [a small coin] that one gives to a poor person one merits and receives the presence of the *Shekhinah*."[7] According to this rabbinic view, the mere giving of *Tzedakah* acts as a catalyst to bring the Divine Presence in contact with the donor.[8] The same interrelationship between the words *Tzedakah* and *Tzedek* is revealed in the following text: "Scripture says: *And it shall be Tzedakah before you* (Deut. 24:13) — you yourself should perform *Tzedakah*. *And it shall be Tzedakah before you* (*ibid.*), this teaches that *Tzedakah* rises before the Throne of Glory and this is what [Scripture] says: *Tzedek shall go before Him as He sets out on His way* (Ps.

---

[6] *Rut Rabbah* 5:9 (on Ruth 2:19).

[7] *Midrash Tehillim* 11:14.

[8] Even during uprisings and wars it was important to give *Tzedakah*, see Arieh Kindler, "A Bar Kokhba Coin Used as a Charity Token," *Israel Numismatic Journal* 12 (1992–93), 73–75.

85:14)."[9] The practice of *Tedakah* places one into a direct relationship with God.

The practice of *Tzedakah* is so powerful that it can affect God. God Himself is not totally independent of human action. With typical rabbinic hyperbole, the Rabbis argue that giving *Tzedakah* can even "save" God.

> "Not only this, but s/he who does justice and *Tzedakah* and preserves many lives … about him/her Scripture says: *He that redeemed my soul with peace* (Ps. 55:19). At the same time, the Holy One, blessed He, asks [rhetorically]: Who ransomed Me and My *Shekhinah* [Divine Presence] and Israel from among the idolatrous nations of the world? It is the one who does justice and *Tzedakah*."[10]

Human acts of *Tzedakah* influence God to protect the donors of *Tzedakah*. One aspect of the power of *Tzedakah* is that it invokes God's infinite power on behalf of those who give *Tzedakah*. This point is emphasized in the rabbinic commentary on the following verse: *May the Lord reward your deeds. May you have a full recompense from the Lord, the God of Israel, under whose wings you have sought refuge!* (Ruth 2:12).

The Rabbis rhetorically questioned who is entitled to this divine protection and they responded:

> "Come and see how great is the power of the *Tzadikim*, and how great is the power of *Tzedakah*, and how great the power of those who do kind deeds, for they obtain shelter neither in the shadow of the morning, nor in the shadow of the wings of the earth, nor in the shadow of the sun, nor in the shadow of the wings of the *ḥayot*, or the cherubim or the seraphim, but under whose wings do they obtain shelter? Under the shadow of Him who spoke and the world was created, as it is written: *How precious is Your loving-kindness, O God! And the children of men take refuge in the shadow of Your wings* (Ps. 36:8)."[11]

---

[9] *Sifré Deut.* 277.

[10] *Seder Eliyahu Rabbah* 11, p. 53, Friedmann edition.

[11] *Rut Rabbah* 5:4.

Although not quoted by the Rabbis, the scriptural citation follows this passage: *Your Tzedakah is like the mighty mountains* (Ps. 36:7). In the rabbinic mind God's *Tzedakah* and *Ḥesed* [loving-kindness] would compel Him to protect those human beings who gave *Tzedakah.* In a very poetic text the Rabbis compare the power of *Tzedakah* to nine other creations of God. Their conclusion is that *Tzedakah* has the greatest power.

> "It has been taught: R. Yudah says: Great is *Tzedakah* in that it brings the redemption nearer, as it is written: *Thus said the Lord: Observe what is right and do Tzedakah; for My salvation shall come, and My deliverance be revealed* (Isa. 56:1). He used to say: The strong things have been created in the world. Rock is hard, but iron cuts it. Iron is hard, but fire softens it. Fire is hard, but water quenches it. Water is strong, but clouds carry it. Clouds are strong, but wind scatters them. Wind is strong, but the body bears it. The body is strong, but fright crushes it. Fright is strong, but wine banishes it. Wine is strong, but sleep works it off. Death is stronger than all, and *Tzedakah* saves from death, as it is written, *Tzedakah delivers from death* (Prov. 10:2)."[12]

In later sections of this chapter, the relationship between *Tzedakah* and death will be investigated. However, for the purposes of this particular unit the above passage again illustrates the tremendous power attributed by the Rabbis to the practice of *Tzedakah.*

RECIPROCITY OF BENEFIT BETWEEN THE DONOR AND THE DONEE

The quality of *Tzedakah* is that it simultaneously bestows a reward upon both the donor and the donee.[13] If one truly appreciates this mutuality of benefit it precludes the donor from having feelings of patronizing the poor. The donor cannot condescend if s/he realiz-

---

[12] *Babylonian Talmud*, Bava Batra 10a.

[13] Marc Hirshman, "On the Nature of Mitzva and its Reward in the *Mishnah* and Tosefta." In: *Proceedings of the Tenth World Congress of Jewish Studies*, Division C, vol. 1 (Jerusalem, World Union of Jewish Studies, 1990), 54–60 (Hebrew).

es that s/he is fortunate to have the opportunity to give *Tzedakah*. In short, giving *Tzedakah* is not a unilateral exchange in which the donor gives something and receives nothing in return. To the contrary, the practice of *Tzedakah* is a bilateral exchange in which both parties mutually benefit.[14]

This concept is illustrated in the Midrashic analysis of the verse in the Book of Ruth in which Naomi and Ruth discuss "gleaning" the field owned by Boaz. (Gleaning itself is a form of *Tzedakah* as described in Tractate *Pe'ah*.) *Her mother-in-law asked her: Where did you glean today? Where did you work? Blessed be he who took such generous notice of you! So she told her mother-in-law the man with whom I worked today is Boaz* (Ruth 2:19). The commentary on this passage is:

> "It was taught in the name of R. Yehoshuʿa: More than the homeowner does for the poor person does the poor person do for the homeowner, for Ruth said to Naomi: *The name of the man with whom I worked today*. She did not say: 'for whom I worked,' but *with whom I worked*. I produced for him many works and benefits in return for the one morsel of food which he fed me."[15]

In receiving *Tzedakah* Ruth did not perceive of herself in a subservient position; she actually provided a greater benefit to Boaz than she herself received. In fact, in the same above rabbinic text it states: "R. Shiloh of Noveh said: Your wealth depends upon the poor man."[16] The person receiving *Tzedakah* enables the donor to retain his wealth. A further example of the simultaneous mutual benefit of *Tzedakah* is evident from the following rabbinic discussion:

> "Another explanation of *If your brother under you continues in straits and must give himself over to you, do not subject him to the treatment of a slave* (Lev. 25:39). This is what is written in Scripture: *The poor*

[14] Partially addressed by Michael Novick, "Charity and reciprocity: structures of benevolence in rabbinic literature," *Harvard Theological Review* 105 (2012), 33–52.

[15] *Rut Rabbah* 5:4.

[16] *Ibid.*

> *person and the oppressor meet together; the Lord gives light to the eyes of both of them* (Prov. 29:13) … If the poor person stands together with the oppressor and says to him/her: Give me *Tzedakah*, and s/he gives it to him/her, then *The Lord gives light to the eyes of both of them* (*ibid.*); the one obtains temporal life and the other the life of the World to Come."[17]

In chapter one of this book the theological concept of God testing the individual is discussed. Within this context of "testing" the one who passes the "test" by giving *Tzedakah* receives rewards during his/her lifetime as well as posthumously. "If the rich person withstands his/her test and practices *Tzedakah*, then s/he will enjoy his/her wealth in this world, while [the reward for his/her good deeds] will be preserved for him/her in the World to Come …"[18]

BENEFITS OBTAINED DURING ONE'S LIFETIME

By giving *Tzedakah* one may obtain Divine Providence. God will look after those individuals who properly fulfill the *mitzvah* of *Tzedakah*. During their lifetimes He will assist them. "Concerning those who are merciful, who feed the hungry, give drink to the thirsty, clothe the naked and distribute *Tzedakot*, Scripture says: *Say you of the Tzadik that it shall be well with him* (Isa. 3:10)."[19]

On a purely material level, giving *Tzedakah* is not a losing proposition. As an incentive for donors, the Rabbis contended that God would replenish any funds expended upon *Tzedakah*. One should give freely, since God would see to it that the donor did not experience a net loss.

> "R. Yitzḥak said: What is the meaning of the verse: *he that followed after Tzedakah and Ḥesed will find life, Tzedakah and honor* (Prov. 21:21)? Because a person has followed after *Tzedakah*, shall s/he find *Tzedakah*? This, however, is to teach you that if a person is eager to give *Tzedakah*, the Holy One, blessed be He, furnished him/her money with which to give it. R.

---

[17] *Vayikra Rabbah* 34:4.

[18] *Shemot Rabbah* 31:3.

[19] *Derekh Eretz Rabbah* 56a.

> Naḥman b. Yitzḥak says: The Holy One, Blessed be He, furnished him/her people who are fitting recipients of *Tzedakah*, so that s/he may be rewarded ..."[20]

The effect of this comment is to minimize any anxieties on the part of the donor. God will provide the money for *Tzedakah* or replace the money already given. Additionally, God will provide the donor with appropriate and deserving donees in order that the donor will be readily rewarded.

One reward that the donor will receive is additional money to enable the donor to continue distributing *Tzedakah*. One's wealth will not be depleted by giving *Tzedakah*, since God will intervene in order to preserve one's capital. However, when God replenishes this wealth, one has a responsibility to give still more *Tzedakah*. "If you have done *Tzedakah*, you will be rewarded with money, and if you are rewarded with money, do *Tzedakah* with your money."[21]

In addition to replenishing his/her wealth the donor of *Tzedakah* may receive even a greater gift from God, namely good health and an increased lifespan. In the following story the donor is given the above rewards since s/he used his/her own personal wealth to help a starving family. S/he did not use as an excuse that the community did not have any funds to help the desperate family.

> "It has been told of Binyamin Ha-Tzadik [the Righteous One] who was an administrator of the communal *Tzedakah* fund: Once a woman came to him in a year of scarcity, and said to him: Rabbi, support me! He said to her: I swear, there is nothing in the *Tzedakah* fund. She said to him: Rabbi, if you do not support me, a woman and her seven children will perish. He stood up and supported her out of his own pocket. Sometime later he became ill and was dying. The angels spoke to the Holy One, blessed be He: Sovereign of the Universe, You said that s/he who preserves one soul of Israel is considered as if s/he preserved the whole world; shall then Binyamin Ha-Tzadik, who has preserved a woman and her seven children die at an early age? At once his sentence [in the Divine Book

---

[20] *Babylonian Talmud*, Bava Batra 9b.

[21] *Derekh Eretz Zutah* 4.

> of Life] was torn up. It has been taught that twenty-two years were added to his life."[22]

Although physical death cannot be completely avoided, *Tzedakah* has the capacity to preclude a donor form dying an untimely, unnatural death. The following passage discusses the famous passage in Proverbs: *Treasures of wickedness profit nothing; but Tzedakah delivers from death* (Prov. 10:2). This verse is interpreted by the Rabbis as delivering one from an unnatural or an evil death. An unnatural death is a premature death such as by accident. An evil death results in the deceased being condemned to *Gehinom*.

> "Does then charity deliver from death? [This refers] to an evil death only."[23] *If your brother is in straits* (Lev. 25:25) — this is what is written: *Happy is he who deals wisely with the poor; the Lord will deliver him in the day of evil* (Ps. 41:2). Abba b. Yirmeah in the name of R. Meir said that is one who lets the Good Inclination rule over the Evil Inclination. R. Isi said this is one who gives a *perutah* to a poor man."[24]

An unnatural death may be avoided if one performs *Tzedakah* in a certain proscribed manner. When is a person delivered from an unnatural death? "When a person gives *Tzedakah* without knowing to whom s/he gives it, and the beggar receives it without knowing from whom s/he receives it … How is a person to do this? S/he should put [his/her money] into the *Tzedakah* box."[25]

THE MIRACLE STORIES

One cannot obtain a true understanding of the rabbinic concept of *Tzedakah* without a familiarity with various "miracle stories" demonstrating the almost transformative quality of *Tzedakah*. This magical or mystical quality of *Tzedakah* can transform a tragedy or disaster into a positive experience. This is demonstrated in the fol-

---

[22] *Babylonian Talmud*, Bava Batra 11a; parallel in *Avot de Rabbi Natan*, 3, version a, Schechter edition.

[23] *Pirke de Rabbi Eliezer* 34, p. 257, Friedlander (trans.).

[24] *Vayikra Rabbah* 34:1.

[25] *Babylonian Talmud*, Bava Batra 10a–b.

lowing rabbinic discussion of the verse *A man's gift makes room for him, and brings him before great men* (Prov. 18:16).

> "Once R. Eliʿezer and R. Yehoshuʿa and R. ʿAkiva went to the Basin of Antiochia[26] to make a collection for scholars. There was one Abba Yudan, who used to generously support [the needy]. He became impoverished, and when he saw our Rabbis there, he went home and his face turned the color of orange-yellow [he was extremely embarrassed]. His wife said to him: Why is your face sickly? He said to her: My Rabbis are here and I do not know what to do. His wife, who was even more righteous than he, said: We have nothing left except the field. Go, sell half of it, and give it to them. The Rabbis prayed for him, saying: May God make good your deficiency!
>
> After a few days he went to plough the half field. The Holy One, blessed be He, gave light to his eyes and the earth broke open and his cow fell and its leg was broken. When he went down to lift it up, he found a treasure under it. He said, my cow's leg was broken, but it turned out to be for my benefit. When our Rabbis came there again, they inquired after him, saying: How is Abba Yudan doing? The neighbors said: He is Abba Yudan of goats, Abba Yudan of donkeys, Abba Yudan of camels.
>
> When he heard [of the arrival of the Rabbis] he went out to meet them and said to them: Your prayer has produced fruit, and fruit from fruit. They said to him: As you live, even though others gave more than you did, we wrote you down at the head [of the list of donors of *Tzedakah*]. Then they took him and gave him a seat among themselves and they applied to

[26] An unidentified location; either the Sandbar of Antiochia or a geological depression near the Springs of Daphne, for the latter explanation see Burton L. Visotzky, *Golden Bells and Pomegranates* (Tübingen: Mohr/Siebeck, 2003), 125–26.

> him this verse: *A man's gift makes room for him, and brings him before great men* (Prov. 18:16)."[27]

The following story also concerns an overly generous contributor of *Tzedakah* who receives material rewards. However, he is such a righteous person that he refuses to benefit from his sudden wealth. He wishes to donate his wealth again to the poor.

> "Whenever the collectors of *Tzedakah* saw R. Eliᶜezer b. Birtah, they would hide themselves from him, because he was in the habit of giving to them all he had. One day he was going to the market to buy a trousseau for his daughter. When the collectors of *Tzedakah* saw him, they hid themselves from him. He ran after them and said to them, What is your business? They replied, A male and female orphan. He said to them: I swear, they take priority over my daughter. And he took all that he had and gave it to them.
>
> He was left with one *zuz* [a small coin] and with this he bought wheat which he deposited in the granary. When his wife returned home she asked her daughter, What did your father bring home? She said, He has put in the granary all that he had bought. She thereupon went to open the door of the granary and she found that it was so full of wheat that the wheat protruded through the hinges of the door-socket and the door would not open because of this.
>
> The daughter went to the *Beit Ha-Midrash* and said to him [her father]: Come and see what your Friend [God] has done for you. Whereupon he said to her, I swear, [the wealth] shall be to you as devoted property, and you shall have no more right to share in it than any poor person in Israel."[28]

---

[27] *Vayikra Rabbah* 5:4; somewhat parallel in *Talmud Yerushalmi*, Horayot 3:4, 48a. Catherine Hezser, *The Social Structure of the Rabbinic Movement in Roman Palestine* (Tübingen: Mohr/Siebeck, 1997), 265, comments that the story assumes that some scholars were as needy as the poor.

[28] *Babylonian Talmud*, Taᶜanit 24a.

Another miracle story emphasizes the theme that God rewards an individual according to his/her deeds. By performing the *mitzvah* of *Tzedakah* one will be amply rewarded. The proof text is Job 34:11 which states: *For He pays a person according to his actions, and provides for him according to his conduct.*

> "There was once a person who had two sons. One of them did a *mitzvah*, but the other did not. The one who did a *mitzvah* sold his house and all that he possessed to do a *mitzvah*. Once on the day of *Hoshaʿna* [the seventh day of Sukkot] his wife gave him ten *pulsing* [small coins] and said to him: Go, buy something in the market for your children. As soon as he went to the market place, the *Tzedakah* collectors met him. They said, Behold, the philanthropist is coming. They then requested him, Give your share in this *mitzvah*, for we wish to buy a garment for an orphan girl. Thereupon he took the money and gave it to them. But he felt ashamed to go [home] to his wife. What did he do?
>
> He went to the synagogue, where he saw some of the *lulavin* [palm branches] carried by the children and the citrons eaten on *Hoshaʿna*. He took some of them and filled his sack and sailed away on the Great Sea until he reached a distant land. When he arrived there, it so happened that the king was suffering from a bowel complaint. His physicians said to him, If you had one of the citrons that the Jews carry on *Hoshaʿna*, you could eat it and be cured. Messengers forthwith went and searched all ships and the whole country, but they found none. They went, however, and found the man lying on his sack. Thereupon they said to him, Have you anything to sell? He replied, I am a poor man, and possess nothing. They then opened his sack and found it full of citrons. They asked him, What are these? He answered, They are citrons that Jews use during the worship service on the day of *Hoshaʿna*.
>
> So they brought him before the king … who ate the citrons and was cured. He then ordered, Empty his sack and fill it with *denari* … Then the king said to him, Make any request, and I shall fulfill it. He replied, I request that my possessions be restored to me and that all the people come forth to meet me. His request was fulfilled. When he reached the harbor, the her-

ald went before him and all the people went forth to meet him, and his brother and his sons also went out to meet him ... It thus came about that when he entered his home, he took possession of his own property and inherited that of his brother, in fulfillment of the verse, *For He pays a person according to his actions, and provides for him according to his conduct* (Job 34:11)."[29]

Even of greater significance than the above material rewards are the stories of a sudden, miraculous avoidance of death. This is illustrated in the Midrashic commentary upon the verse: *Cast your bread upon the waters, for you shall find it after many days* (Eccl. 11:1).

"R. Bibi said: If you wish to do *Tzedakah*, do it upon those who labor in the Torah, because the 'waters' said here are nothing else but the words of the Torah, as it is said: *Ho, every one that is thirsty come you for water, and he that does not have money: Come, buy and eat; yes, come buy wine and milk without money and without price* (Isa. 55:1).

R. ʿAkiva said: When I was travelling at sea, I saw a ship which had sunk, and I was concerned about a *Talmid Ḥakham* [student] who had been on board and drowned. When I came to the province of Cappadocia, I noticed him sitting before me and asking questions. I said to him: My son, how did you raise up from the sea? He said: Rabbi, through your prayer on my behalf one wave tossed me to another, and another to another until they brought me ashore. I said to him: My son, what good deed do you possess? He answered: When I went aboard the ship, a poor person met me and said: Help me!, and I gave him a loaf. He said to me, As you have restored my life to me by your gift, so will your life be restored to you. [R. ʿAkiva

---

[29] *Vayikra Rabbah* 37:2. See also Michael L. Satlow, "'Fruit and the fruit of fruit': charity and piety among Jews in Late Antique Palestine," *Jewish Quarterly Review* 100, 2 (2010), 244–77; Avigdor Shinan, "The Tale of the Citrons," *Meḥkere Yerushalayim be-folklor yehudi* 13/14 (1990/91), 61–79 (Hebrew).

> said:] For him I have read the verse: *Cast your bread upon the waters; for you shall find it after many days* (Eccl. 11:1)."[30]

Still another story about a miraculous rescue at sea has a very similar theme to the above episode.

> "A story about a pious man who was habitually charitable. One time he set out in a boat; a wind arose and sank the boat in the sea. Rabbi ʿAkiva saw this and came before the court to testify that his wife might remarry. Before he could testify, the man came and stood before him.
>
> [R. ʿAkiva] said to him: Are you not the one who drowned in the sea?
>
> [The man] said: Yes.
>
> And who raised you out of the sea?
>
> The *Tzedakah* which I practiced raised me out of the sea.
>
> How do you know this?
>
> He said to him: When I sank to the depth of the sea, I heard the sound of a great noise of the waves of the sea, one wave saying to the other and the other to another: Hurry! And let us raise this man out of the sea, for he practices *Tzedakah* all of his days.
>
> Rabbi ʿAkiva explained: Blessed be God, the God of Israel, who has chosen the words of the Torah and the words of the Sages, for the words of the Torah and the words of the Sages are established forever and ever, for it is written, *Cast your bread upon the waters, for you shall find it after days* (Eccl. 11:1); furthermore, it is written: *Tzedakah delivers from death* (Prov. 10:2)."[31]

---

[30] *Kohelet Rabbah* 11:1,1.

[31] *Avot de Rabbi Natan* 3, version a, Schechter edition. Menachem Ben-Shalom, "Matan Tsedakah shel Ḥasidim le-or Avot de Rabbi Natan nusaḥ aleph." In: Yuval Shahar, ed., *Festschrift Arieh Kasher* (Tel-Aviv, 2012), 275–94 (Hebrew).

As can be seen, R. ᶜAkiva frequently plays a key role in these miraculous stories concerning *Tzedakah*. Evidently R. ᶜAkiva taught his daughter the value of giving *Tzedakah* since her life was saved as a result of helping a poor man.

> "From R. ᶜAkiva we also [learn that] there is no planetary influence over Israel. For R. ᶜAkiva had a daughter. Chaldeans [astrologers] told him: On the day that she enters the bridal chamber a snake will bite her and she will die. He was very worried about this. On that day she took a brooch, stuck it into the wall and by chance it sank into the eyes of a serpent. The following morning, when she took it out, the snake was trailing after it. What did you do? Her father said. She said: A poor man came to our door in the evening and everybody was busy at the banquet, and there was none to listen to him. He said to her: You have done a good deed. R. ᶜAkiva went out and lectured: *But Tzedakah delivers from death* (Prov. 10:2) — and not [merely] from an unnatural death, but from death itself."[32]

The last sentence in the above passage is probably rabbinic hyperbole. *Tzedakah* cannot bring one immortality; however, it can postpone the inevitable and also can preclude one from a premature death. Louis Ginzberg in a note concerning the Talmudic passage contends that the beggar at the door may have been the angel of death who was prevented to fulfill his mission of bringing death to the daughter of R. ᶜAkiva.[33]

BENEFITS IN THE WORLD TO COME

The Rabbis were well aware that not all those who gave *Tzedakah* prospered during their lifetimes and enjoyed good health and long lives. Consequently, it was important to the Rabbis that *Tzedakah* provide numerous benefits in the afterlife. During one's lifetime one should not concern oneself only with the temporal life; one should also devote one's energies to securing a desirable fate in the

---

[32] *Babylonian Talmud*, Shabbat 156b.

[33] Ginzberg, *The Legends of the Jews*, 7 vols. (Philadelphia: The Jewish Publication Society, 1949), vol. 6, p. 336, n. 96.

World to Come. This attitude is exemplified in the following passage:

> "Our Rabbis taught a story of King Monobaz that he dissipated all of his own wealth and the wealth of his father in years of scarcity. His brothers and his father's household came in a group to him and said to him: Your father saved money and added [to the treasures] of his fathers, and you dissipated them. He said: My father saved up below and I am saving up above, as it says: *Truth springs out of the earth and Tzedek looks down from heaven* (Ps. 85:12). My fathers stored something which produces not fruits, but I have stored something which does produce fruits, as it says: *Say you of the righteous [Tzadik] that it shall be well with them, for they shall eat of the fruit of their doings* (Isa. 3:10). My fathers saved treasures of money, but I have saved treasures of souls, as it says: *The fruit of the righteous [Tzadik] is a tree of life, and he that is wise wins souls* (Prov. 11:30). My father gathered for others and I have gathered for myself, as it says: *And for you it shall be Tzedakah* (Deut. 24:13). My father gathered for this world but I have gathered for the World to Come, as it says: *Your Tzedakah shall go before you, and the glory of the Lord shall be behind you* (Isa. 58:8)."[34]

The Rabbis were extremely concerned about avoiding the judgment of being condemned to *Gehinom*. *Gehinom* was reserved for those who failed to atone for their sins, for those who failed to do *Tzedakah*. To escape from *Gehinom* was an ample reward for performing *Tzedakah*.

To reinforce this point, the Rabbis were willing to twist the literal meaning of Scripture. In a difficult passage in which the Hebrew is uncertain, the Rabbis gave the following translation to serve their purposes: *Thus says the Lord, though they be in full strength and likewise many, even so shall they be sheared off, and he shall cross* (Nah. 1:12). The interpretation of this verse is as follows:

> "If a person sees that his/her livelihood is insufficient, s/he should do *Tzedakah* from it, and all the more so if it is plenti-

---

[34] *Babylonian Talmud*, Bava Batra 11a.

> ful. What is the meaning of the words, *Even so shall they be sheared off and he shall cross?* In the school of R. Yishma'el it was taught: Whoever shears off part of his possessions and does *Tzedakah* from it, is delivered from the punishment of *Gehinom.* A simile of two sheep crossing a river, one shorn and the other not shorn; the shorn one gets across, the unshorn one does not, *And though I have afflicted you* (Nah. 1:12) — Mar Zutra said: Even a poor man who himself subsists on *Tzedakah* should give *Tzedakah*; *I will afflict you no more* (*ibid.*) — R. Yosef taught: If he does that, [God] will not again show him signs of poverty."[35]

By practicing *Tzedakah* one obtains an advocate in the World to Come. "It is like a man who had some trouble with the king and who had defenders who pleaded for him to the king. Similarly, when a man fulfills the commandments, and studies Torah and practices *Tzedakah*, then while Satan stands accusing him, his defenders stand opposite pointing out his good deeds, as it says: *A man's gifts makes room for him* (Prov. 18:16). What he has done for the poor helps towards this; it says: *Happy is he that considers the poor* (Ps. 41:2)."[36]

Consequently, we have that famous saying that is repeated at the time of Rosh Ha-Shanah and Yom Kippur:

> "For R. Yudan said in the name of R. Eliᶜezer: Three things annul evil decrees, these are *Tefilah* [prayer], *Tzedakah* and *Teshuvah* [repentance], and the three of them are mentioned in one verse, as it is written: *If my people, upon whom My name is called, shall humble themselves, and pray, and seek My face, and turn from their evil ways; then will I hear from heaven, and will forgive their sin, and will heal their land* (2 Chron. 7:14). *And pray*, that is prayer; *and seek My face*, that is *Tzedakah*, as it is said: *I shall behold Your face in righteousness* (Ps. 17:15); *And turn from their evil ways*, that is repentance."[37]

---

[35] *Babylonian Talmud*, Gittin 7a–b.

[36] *Shemot Rabbah* 31:2.

[37] *Kohelet Rabbah* 5:1,6; parallel in *Pesikta de Rav Kahana* 28.

By performing the *mitzvah* of *Tzedakah* one can annul the evil decree that would relegate one to *Gehinom*. Instead, if God wills it, one may be granted access to Heaven. The Gates of the Righteous, the entryway to Heaven, will be opened to those who have given *Tzedakah*. In commenting upon the verse, *Open the Gates of Righteousness for me* (Ps. 118:19), the Rabbis stated in the World to Come everyone will be asked:

> "What was your occupation? If the person answers, I used to feed the hungry, they will say to him, This is God's gate; you, who fed the hungry, may enter. I used to give water to those who were thirsty, they will say to him, This is God's gate, you, who gave water to those who were thirsty, may enter. I used to clothe the naked, they will say to him, This is God's gate, you, who clothed the naked, may enter. And similarly with those who raised orphans, and who did *Tzedakah*, and who performed acts of caring, and loving-kindness."[38]

Thus for the rabbinic mind *Tzedakah* provided one with an opportunity to gain immortality. One should never underestimate the benefits that one could attain by giving *Tzedakah*. A sufficiently generous person may enter the World to Come; eternal life may be the ultimate reward of *Tzedakah*. One who learned this lesson was R. Tarfon.

> "It was said of R. Tarfon that he was very wealthy but did not give gifts to the poor. R. ʿAkiva once found him and said, My teacher, would you like me to purchase a city or two for you? R. Tarfon replied, Yes, and he immediately gave him four thousand gold *denari*. R. ʿAkiva took the money and distributed it to the poor. A while later, R. Tarfon found him and said, Where are the cities you purchased for me? He took him by the hand and brought him to the *Beit Ha-Midrash*. He then took a copy of the Book of Psalms and placed it in front of them. They read and read, until they came to the verse, *He gives freely to the poor, his Tzedakah endures forever* (Ps. 112:9). R. ʿAkiva said to him, This is the city I bought for you! R. Tarfon arose

---

[38] *Midrash Tehillim* 118:17.

and kissed him and said, My teacher, my hero! My teacher in wisdom! My hero in the essences of life! He then gave him more money to give away."[39]

[39] *Kallah Rabbati* 52b.

CHAPTER FOUR: THE PENALTY OF NOT GIVING *TZEDAKAH*

Tzedakah has the capacity to bring the donor into a direct relationship with God. Conversely, for those who fail to give *Tzedakah* the relationship with God is severed. For the rabbinic mind one determinant of the existence of such a close relationship with God was whether or not everyone's prayers were answered. They offered the explanation that those individuals who did not practice *Tzedakah* were punished by God. He would no longer respond to their prayers. Surely, this is viewed as one of the most severe penalties that God could enact.

In analyzing the verse: *And money answers all things* (Eccl. 10:19) the Rabbis commented:

> R. Yehoshuʿa of Sikhnin said in the name of R. Levi: Sometimes a man's prayer is answered, and sometimes it is not. At those times when he used [his money] for *Tzedakah* he is answered, as it is said, *So shall my Tzedakah answer for me* (Gen. 30:33); but at those times when he does not use [his money] for *Tzedakah*, it is used as an accusation against him, as it is written: *To testify against him* (Deut. 16:19)."[1]

One prayer that virtually every parent must utter is for the welfare of her/his children. Yet, if one fails to give *Tzedakah* that prayer will not be answered. Indeed, the child may be punished for the sin of the parent. This point is illustrated in the sad story of a daughter of a wealthy man. Her father did not appreciate his social responsibilities as a man of wealth. Consequently, he brought tragedy upon himself and his family.

---

[1] *Kohelet Rabbah* 10:1, 19.

> "Our Rabbis taught: A story of R. Yoḥanan b. Zakai who was riding on a donkey and leaving Jerusalem, while his disciples followed him. He saw a girl picking barley grains in the dung of Arab cattle. When she saw him she wrapped herself in her hair and stood before him. She said to him: Rabbi, support me! He said to her: My daughter, who are you? She said: I am the daughter of Nakdimon b.Gorion. He said to her: My daughter, where did the wealth of your father's house go? She said: Is there not a proverb in Jerusalem: The salt of money is diminution?"

The preservation of money is enabled by the practice of *Tzedakah* which temporarily decreases one's wealth but simultaneously acts to preserve it. This interpretation of the above proverb is based upon the final word being *ḥaser*, to lessen or decrease "And some say *Ḥesed*." The preservation of wealth occurs as a result of the performance of benevolent deeds. This interpretation of the above proverb is based upon the final word being *Ḥesed*. The text is unclear as to whether the last (Hebrew) letter of the word in question is the letter *Resh* or *Dalet*, which have similar shapes.

> "And where is the wealth of your father-in-law's house? She said, The one [Roman enemy] came and destroyed the other. Do you remember, Rabbi, when you signed my *Ketubah*? He said to his disciples: I remember that when I signed her *Ketubah*, I read in it: A million gold *denari* from her father's house in addition to [the money] from her father-in-law's house. Rabban Yoḥanan b. Zakai wept and said: How happy are Israel! When they do God's will, no nation and no language has any power over them, but when they do not do God's will, He gives them into the hands of a low nation, and not only into the hands of a low nation but into the power of the beasts of a low nation.
>
> Nakdimon b. Gorion did not practice *Tzedakah*. Has it not been taught: It was said of Nakdimon b. Gorion that woolen clothes were spread under his feet when he left his house and the poor followed him and folded them up. If you want, I

> might answer: He did it for his glorification. And if you want, I might answer: He did not act as he should have done. As people say: The burden is in accordance with the camel."[2]

The proverb in the above text means that the greater the strength of the camel, the greater the burden that it may carry. Thus the greater one's wealth, the greater one's obligation to perform *Tzedakah* in a socially responsible manner. In the above story, Nakdimon b. Gorion merely left behind some woolen garments wherever he walked. Given his great wealth this was an insignificant act. Furthermore, it was given in a manner contemptuous of the poor. Subsequently, he lost his fortune and his daughter was reduced to penury. Extreme poverty was not the only penalty that one could suffer if one ignored the *mitzvah* of *Tzedakah*. One could lose one's good health which is an even more precious commodity.

In explicating the verse: *I went down into the garden of nuts* (Song 6:11) the Rabbis made the following analogy concerning *Tzedakah*: "Just as there are soft nuts, medium nuts, and exceedingly hard nuts, so in Israel there are those who give *Tzedakah* of their own free will, those who have to be asked before they give, and those who do not give even when asked. R. Levi said: The proverb says: The door that is not opened for good deeds will be opened for the physician."[3] Thus the failure to give *Tzedakah* could lead to ill health or even death.

In the above cases the penalty for noncompliance with the commandment of *Tzedakah* was imposed upon the individual him/herself who failed to act or upon his/her immediate family. However, in some instances the community at large could suffer as well. For example, in the agrarian society of ancient Israel rain was a necessity. In the *Shmoneh Esreh* [the "Eighteen Benedictions"] there is a special acknowledgement of God's capacity to cause the wind to blow and the rain to fall, which is recited between *Sukkot* and *Pesaḥ*. A drought was perceived as a community trauma. What could be the explanation for such severe punishment by God?

---

[2] *Babylonian Talmud*, Ketubbot 66b–67a.

[3] *Shir Ha-Shirim Rabbah* 6:1, 11; parallel in *Pesikta Rabbati* 11:7, Ulmer ed.

"And R. Yoḥanan said: Rain is withheld only on account of those who subscribe to *Tzedakah* in public and do not give it, as it is said, *As vapours and wind without rain, so is he that boasts himself of a false gift* (Prov. 25:14)."[4] In both instances the wind and the braggart act deceitfully and disappoint one's reasonable expectations. In the rabbinic view God imposed a terrible sanction upon a community when an individual member of said community failed to honor his/her pledge of *Tzedakah*. With this perspective there would naturally be tremendous social pressure for each member of a community to keep his/her commitment in respect to any public statement concerning *Tzedakah*.

The same point as above is made in the rabbinic explanation of why there was famine in the days of King David. The Rabbis enumerated five sins that were the cause of the rains not falling in the days of David, among them: "Because of the sin of those who publicly subscribe to *Tzedakah* and do not give it."[5] In chapter eleven there will be a further discussion of the interrelationship between public vows and *Tzedakah*.

---

[4] *Babylonian Talmud*, Taʿanit 8b.

[5] *Bemidbar Rabbah* 8:4.

CHAPTER FIVE: THE ROLE OF *TZEDAKAH* IN THE COMMUNITY

As can be seen from the preceding chapter, the penalty of not giving *Tzedakah* can impact adversely upon a community. With the same rationale, the practice of *Tzedakah* can benefit a community. The greatest benefit that a community could receive is that of the physical survival of its youth, without whom it has no future.

A certain community was in anguish over the early demise of its youthful population. The remedy to reverse this pattern was *Tzedakah*:

> "A story of two families of priests who came before Raban Yoḥanan b. Zakai and said to him: Rabbi, our sons die at the age of twelve. He replied: Are you from the family of Eli's descendants to whom it was said, *All the increase of your house shall die young men* (1 Sam. 2:33)? They said: Rabbi, what are we to do? He replied: When any son of yours reaches puberty, estimate his worth and then give *Tzedakah,* keeping in mind the verse: *Tzedakah delivers from death* (Prov. 10:2). You will thus save from death a descendant of Eli to whom it was said, *All the increase of your house shall die young men* (1 Sam. 2:33). So the families did as they were advised and thus delivered themselves from death."[1]

The practice of *Tzedakah* encouraged the individual to go beyond the self, to have a social awareness, to have compassion and empathy. These values are exemplified in the following rabbinic typology:

---

[1] *Seder Eliyahu Rabah* 11, p. 53, Friedmann edition.

> "There are four types among people: one that says, What is mine is mine and what is yours is yours — this is the common type, and some say that this is the type of Sodom. Sodom was destroyed not because people committed evil acts but merely because they were indifferent to the suffering of others. One that says, What is mine is yours and what is yours is mine — he is an ignorant person. One that says, What is mine is yours and what is yours is your own — is a *Ḥasid*. And one that says, What is yours is mine, and what is mine is mine own — is a wicked person."[2]

One not only had a social responsibility to others in respect to *Tzedakah*, one had an affirmative obligation to encourage the practice of *Tzedakah* among one's neighbors. It was the Rabbis' intention to foster the practice of *Tzedakah* within a community as can be gleaned from the following quotation: "There are four types of characters who give *Tzedakah*: One who gives and wants others to give is a *Ḥasid*. One who does not give and does not want others to give is a villain. One who gives but does not want others to give has a bad reputation. One who does not give and wants others to give has a bad reputation."[3]

Thus *Tzedakah* should not be practiced in isolation but rather within the context of a community in which all members contribute their respective share. It is a great deed to facilitate the giving of *Tzedakah* by others. "R. Eleʿazar said: He who causes others to do good is greater than the doer, as it says, *And the work of Tzedakah shall be peace, and the effect of Tzedakah quiet and confidence forever* (Isa. 32:17)."[4]

In the process of elevating the individual, the practice of *Tzedakah* has the potential of ennobling the entire community. *Tzedakah* reaches its greatest potential in the context of a community-wide effort. "What is the meaning of the verse *And he put on Tzedakah as a coat of mail* (Isa. 59:17)? It tells you that just as in a coat of mail every small scale joins with the others into one piece of armor, so

[2] *Avot de Rabbi Natan*, 40, version a, Schechter edition.

[3] *Avot de Rabbi Natan*, 45, version b, Schechter edition.

[4] *Babylonian Talmud*, Bava Batra 9a.

likewise every *perutah* given to *Tzedakah* joins with the rest into a large sum. R. Ḥanina said: From here, *And all our Tzedakah is a polluted garment* (Isa. 64:5). Just as in a garment every thread joins with the rest into a whole garment, so every *perutah* given to *Tzedakah* joins with the rest to form a large sum."[5]

One should never minimize the significance of the act of *Tzedakah*. Even though one's individual contribution may be small, it nevertheless serves as another thread in a gigantic tapestry. Each human being has the potential of being an artisan in this magnificent work of art; a world in which *Tzedakah* is universally practiced. Only through the efforts of the community is *Tzedakah* capable of creating such a masterpiece.

Tzedakah entails communal responsibility. Thus the Rabbis make the legal inquiry of how long does one need to be a resident in a town before one's communal obligation commence. Their answer; "Thirty days to become liable for contributing to the *tamḥui*, three months for the *kupah*, six months for the clothing fund, nine months for the burial fund, and twelve months for contributing to the repair of town walls."[6] This text bears two critical words that are essential to comprehending the communal nature of *Tzedakah*, namely *tamḥui* and *kupah*. These critical terms were defined by Mordecai Kaplan:

> "Prescribed methods for collecting and distributing funds are known to have existed even before the destruction of the second Temple in the year 70. Two types of funds in particular survived from that early period almost to our own day. They were known as *kupah* and *tamḥui*. *Kupah* was the community chest made up of weekly money collections. Thence the local poor were provided with their necessaries for at least a week's time. Thence too provisions were made for the support of orphan children. When a poor couple married, the husband would have his rent paid, and the wife would receive her clothing outfit from this *kupa*. The *tamḥui* consisted of the weekly collections not in money but in kind. That served as a sort of

---

[5] *Babylonian Talmud*, Bava Batra 9b.

[6] *Babylonian Talmud*, Bava Batra 8a.

> emergency supply for the vagrant poor and also for the resident poor who needed food immediately."[7]

Kaplan mentions the special category of orphans. Although they were recipients in the above explanation, they could also become donors. Virtually no one is exempt from the duty of giving *Tzedakah*. "Rava levied a contribution for *Tzedakah* on the house of Bar Merion. Abaye said to him: Has not R. Shmuʾel b. Yehudah taught that money for *Tzedakah* is not to be levied on orphans even for the redemption of captives? He said: I collect from them in order to give them a better standing."[8] In this passage it is important to note that *Tzedakah* could be levied upon individuals to serve the communal needs. Thus *Tzedakah* should not be construed as a purely voluntary act by an individual. The price of being a member of a community included the payment of *Tzedakah*. Furthermore, it should be noted that Rava's justification for levying upon even orphans was to elevate their social status. If one failed to give *Tzedakah*, irrespective of the amount, one had little social standing.

As explained earlier (chapter three), *Tzedakah* has the unique capacity to elevate the donor as well as the recipient. Without having the ability to give *Tzedakah* one's self-respect may be diminished. Consequently, even the poor should give *Tzedakah*. "Mar Zutra said: Even a poor person who subsists on *Tzedakah* should give *Tzedakah*."[9]

Tzedakah was an essential and integral part of the Jewish life in a community. In some small Jewish communities there was not a sufficient number of Jews to effectively practice *Tzedakah*. In such an isolated enclave Jewish scholars were prohibited from residing. "It has been taught: A scholar should not reside in a city where the following ten things are not found: A *Beit Din* that imposes flagellation and decrees penalties; a *kupah* collected by two and distributed by three; a synagogue; a public toilet; a circumciser; a surgeon; an

---

[7] Mordecai M. Kaplan, "Jewish Philanthropy: Traditional and Modern." In: E. Farris, F. Laune, and A. Todd (eds.), *Intelligent Philanthropy* (Chicago, 1930), pp. 52–89, 59.

[8] *Babylonian Talmud*, Bava Batra 8a.

[9] *Babylonian Talmud*, Gittin 7b.

artist versed in calligraphy; a ritual slaughterer and a teacher."[10] Although the above list may not have been written in order of importance, it is interesting to note that *kupah* was written even before synagogue.

[10] *Babylonian Talmud*, Sanhedrin 17b.

CHAPTER SIX: THE URGENCY OF GIVING *TZEDAKAH*

Most *mitzvot* should be done at the earliest possible opportunity. For example, the *mitzvah* of *brit milah* is traditionally performed early in the morning of the eighth day after birth. This principle is especially true in respect to the practice of *Tzedakah.* Poverty, as was discussed in chapter two, was omnipresent during the rabbinic age. The Rabbis were fully aware that the prompt performance of *Tzedakah* could result in the saving of human life.

Nevertheless, a rabbinic debate was held as to whether or not an investigation should be conducted prior to the distribution of either food or clothing. Perhaps, since both commodities were in short supply the Rabbis were concerned about inadvertently giving *Tzedakah* to an undeserving donee. This point will be explored in chapter sixteen. In any event, the Rabbis divided themselves into two schools of thought about the necessity of a prior investigation in respect to giving away food and clothing. One school of thought held that an investigation should be conducted concerning food distribution and not in respect to the giving of clothing. Not surprisingly, the other school of thought had the converse position.

One scriptural verse that was utilized for rabbinic analysis was Isa. 58:7 which states: *It is to share your bread with the hungry, and to take the wretched poor into your home; when you see the naked, to clothe him, and not to ignore your own kin*. In respect to the second clause in the above verse "R. Ada bar Ahavah and R. Yoḥanan held differing views. One says, in regard to clothing, the applicant is investigated carefully but not in regard to food. The wise say that also in regard to clothing there should be no investigation, on account of the

Covenant of Abraham. *And not to ignore your own kin* (*ibid.*), Bar Kappara said you must regard the poor man's flesh as if it were your own."[1] The reference to the Covenant of Abraham implies that the presence or absence of evidence of circumcision should not be exposed.

The Rabbis have an almost infinite capacity to see many aspects of the same issue. For example, R. Huna is sensitive to the fact that naked people or those in rags are subject to contempt and that hunger is usually not as visible as nakedness. Using this rationale, he argues that clothing should be distributed immediately while questions may be asked in regard to those claiming to be hungry. However, R. Yudah contends that those without food are actually suffering while those without clothing are not in such acute distress.[2] Although the above debate did not resolve the issue, it demonstrates that the urgency of giving *Tzedakah* sometimes resulted in the elimination of even a cursory examination of the individual seeking assistance.

Another concern of the Rabbis was whether one should give *Tzedakah* in the form of money or in kind. The problem with giving money was that it would not lead to instant relief to the poor. The money had to be converted into actual necessities that were craved by the destitute. For example, "A wife stays at home and gives bread to the poor which they can at once enjoy while I give them money which they cannot at once enjoy."[3]

A delay in giving *Tzedakah*, even for an instant, may be the difference between life and death. This is tragically depicted in the explanation of the many calamities in the life of Naḥum of Gamzu who was blind in both eyes, his two hands and legs were amputated, and his whole body was covered with boils and he was lying in a dilapidated house on a bed the feet of which were standing in bowls of water in order to prevent the ants from crawling on him.

> "And his disciple said to him, Rabbi, since you are wholly righteous, why has all this come upon you? And he said, I have

---

[1] *Vayikra Rabbah* 34:14, Romm edition.

[2] *Babylonian Talmud*, Bava Batra 9a.

[3] *Babylonian Talmud*, Ta'anit 23b.

> brought it all on myself. Once I was journeying on the road and was travelling to the house of my father-in-law and I had with me three donkeys, one laden with food, one with drink, and one with all kinds of delicacies, when a poor man approached me and stopped me on the road and said to me, Master, give me something to eat. I replied to him, Wait until I have unloaded something from the donkey; I had hardly unloaded something from the donkey when the man died from hunger. I then went and laid myself on him and exclaimed, May my eyes which had no pity upon your eyes become blind, May my hands which has no pity upon your hands be cut off, May my legs which had no pity upon your legs be amputated, and my mind was not at rest until I added, May my whole body be covered with boils. His students declared, Alas! That is why we see you in such a sore plight. To this he said, Woe would it be to me did you not see me in such a sore plight."[4]

Another consideration of the Rabbis was the urgency of life itself. Each one of us has only a finite existence upon the earth. We should number our days wisely by devoting our lives to the performance of *mitzvot*, especially that of giving *Tzedakah.*

> "It was further taught, R. Shimᶜon b. Eleᶜazar said: Do justice and *Tzedakah* while you can find a recipient of your *Tzedakah*, have the opportunity, and it is yet in your power. Solomon in his wisdom said: *Remember then your Creator in the days of your youth, before the evil days come* (Eccl. 12:1) — this refers to the days of old age; *And the years draw nigh, when you shall say: I have no pleasure in them* (*ibid.*) — this refers to the Messianic era, wherein there is neither merit nor guilt."[5]

Since life is precarious, uncertain and of short duration there is an urgency to life itself. The giving of *Tzedakah* should not be deferred to a later date since the opportunity to perform *Tzedakah* may not be possible at that time.

---

[4] *Babylonian Talmud*, Taʾanit 21a.

[5] *Babylonian Talmud*, Shabbat 151b.

CHAPTER SEVEN: GIVING *TZEDAKAH* DISCREETLY AND INDIRECTLY

The quality of the reward is dependent upon how the act of *Tzedakah* was performed. For example, if *Tzedakah* is given discreetly the reward would be much greater than if the *Tzedakah* was given indiscreetly. For the rabbinic mind an indiscreet act of *Tzedakah* virtually nullified the *mitzvah* of performing *Tzedakah*. Discretion was essential in order not to embarrass the recipient. It should be noted that many Jewish communities during the rabbinic period were small enough that virtually all Jews knew one another within the community. To avoid embarrassing the donee it was preferable to give the *Tzedakah* anonymously in order that the recipient would not be humbled in the presence of his benefactor. Ideally, the poor individual could walk in dignity among his townspeople and never know who among them was assisting him with the necessities of life. However, human curiosity would on occasion interfere with the above idealistic paradigm.

> "Mar ᶜUkba had a poor man in his neighborhood for whom he used to throw every day four *zuz* upon his door-step. One day [the poor individual] said: I shall go and see who does this good act for me. On the same day it occurred that Mar ᶜUkba was late in the *Beit Midrash* and his wife came home with him. When the poor man saw them he went after them, but they ran away from him into a furnace, from which the fire had just been extinguished. Mar ᶜUkba's feet were burning and his wife spoke to him: Raise your feet and put them on mine … And what is [the reason for] all this? Because Mar Zutra b. Tuviah said in the name of Rav … It is more becoming for a man that he throws himself into a fiery furnace than publicly put his neighbor to shame. From where do we derive this? From

> Tamar, for it is written, *When she was brought forth* (Gen. 38:25)."[1]

In order to understand the above biblical citation it is necessary to refer to the context in Gen. 38:24–25: *And it came to pass about three months after, that it was told Judah, saying: Tamar your daughter-in-law has played the harlot and moreover, behold, she is with child by harlotry. And Judah said: Bring her forth, and let her be burnt. When she was brought forth, she sent to her father-in-law, saying: By the man, whose these are, I am with child, and she said: Discern, I pray you, whose are these, the signet, the cords, and the staff.* The Rabbis interpreted this passage as a decision by Tamar to be burned to death rather than to publicly humiliate her father-in-law by disclosing their sexual tryst. In order to avoid shaming Judah she sent him a private message. Only through Judah's public acknowledgement of their liaison was Tamar saved (Gen. 38:26). From the above rabbinical understanding of the Tamar story Mar Zutra extrapolated that it was better to die a fiery death than to embarrass a recipient of *Tzedakah.*

In a similar rabbinic hyperbole is the following text which emphasizes the importance of *Tzedakah.* "R. Eleᶜazar said: A man who gives *Tzedakah* in secret is greater than Moses our Teacher, for of Moses it is written, *For I was in dread of the anger and the hot displeasure* (Deut. 9:19), and of the one who gives *Tzedakah* [secretly] it is written, *A gift in secret pacifies anger* (Prov. 21:14)."[2] By inference, the Rabbis reasoned that since a secret gift can subdue anger, the one who practices discreet *Tzedakah* is even more powerful than Moses who was incapable of subduing God's fierce wrath.

For the Rabbis, every human action, whether overt or covert, was constantly being monitored by God. One could not escape the purview of God as acknowledged in the following biblical verse: *For God shall bring every work into the judgment concerning every hidden thing, whether it be good or whether it be evil* (Eccl. 12:14). In commenting upon the last clause in the above verse:

> "The School of R. Yannai said: This refers to one who gives alms to a poor person publicly [an apparent good deed which

[1] *Babylonian Talmud*, Ketubbot 67b.

[2] *Babylonian Talmud*, Bava Batra 9b.

> is really inappropriate, "evil"] like [the story] of R. Yannai. He saw a man give a *zuz* to a poor person publicly, so he said to him: It had been better that you had not given him, than that you have given him publicly and put him to shame. The School of R. Shila said: This refers to one who gives alms to a woman secretly, for he brings her into suspicion."[3]

Thus we see the subtle sensitivity of the Rabbis. Not every secret act of *Tzedakah* is meritorious. The vivid imagination of the Rabbis construed a hypothetical situation in which the secret performance of *Tzedakah* could conceivably embarrass the recipient. If discovered, the woman who had been secretly receiving the money from a man may be deemed to be a prostitute in the eyes of her neighbors. Whether to give *Tzedakah* publicly or in secret depends upon the particular circumstances of the individual case. However, the general preference of the Rabbis is in favor of secret *Tzedakah*. It is more appropriate for certain human conduct to be performed in a modest, private setting. What activity could be more private than human sexuality? The erotic poetry of the Song of Songs had to be interpreted on a more spiritual plane. For example, the following passage was construed as supporting discreet *Tzedakah*: *How beautiful are your steps in sandals, O prince's daughter! The roundings of your thighs are like the links of a chain, the work of your hands of a skilled workman* (Song 7:2). The phrase *the roundings of your thighs* denotes something that should only be seen by one's lover. Similarly, *Tzedakah* should only be seen by God.[4]

Parallel to the concept of giving *Tzedakah* discreetly is the concept of giving *Tzedakah* indirectly. For example, one could enable individuals to escape from the humiliation of receiving *Tzedakah* publicly. This was the common fate of orphans. By raising the orphan in one's home one could still practice *Tzedakah*, but in an indirect manner. This is illustrated in the following text: *Happy are they that keep justice, that do Tzedakah at all times* (Ps. 106:3). "R. Shmu'el b. Naḥmani said: This refers to a man who brings up an

---

[3] *Babylonian Talmud*, Ḥagigah 5a; parallel in *Kohelet Rabbah* 12:1,14.

[4] *Babylonian Talmud*, Mo'ed Katan 16b.

orphan boy or orphan girl in his house and enables them to marry."[5]

Another indirect approach to *Tzedakah* would be to convert an event into an act of *Tzedakah* even though that was not the original intent of the parties.

> "One day Abaye sent to [Abba the Cupper] two scholars in order to test him. He received them and gave them food and drink and in the evening he prepared woolen mattresses for them. In the morning the scholars rolled these together and took them to the market [for sale]. There they met [Abba the Cupper] and they said to him, Sir, value these, how much are they worth? And he replied, So-and-so much. They said to him, Perhaps they are worth more? He said, This is what I paid for them. They then said to him, They are yours, we took them away from you, tell us, please, of what did you suspect us? He replied, I said to myself, perhaps the Rabbis needed the money to redeem captives and they were ashamed to tell me. They replied, Sir, take them back. He answered, From the moment I missed them, I dismissed them from my mind and [I gave them] to *Tzedakah*."[6]

Another method of indirect *Tzedakah* was that of honorable deception. The donor deceives the recipient in order to avoid embarrassing him. The donee is not aware that he is receiving *Tzedakah*.

> "R. Yonah said: It is not written 'Happy is the person that gives to the poor' but *Happy is the person that considers the poor* (Ps. 41:1), [which means] how to benefit him. R. Yonah, when he saw a person from an honorable family who had lost his money and was ashamed to take *Tzedakah*, used to go to him and say to him: As I have heard that you have come into an inheritance in a city abroad, I offer you this thing, and when you have some income you will give it back to me. At the same time when he gave it to him, he would say to him: I have given it to you as a gift. R. Levi in the name of R. Ḥama b. R. Ḥanina

---

[5] *Babylonian Talmud*, Ketubbot 50a.

[6] *Babylonian Talmud*, Ta'anit 21b–22a.

> said: *happy* (Ps. 41:1) is written twenty-two times [in conjunction with some meritorious deed] and "compensation" is only mentioned in one instance. What compensation is offered? *Happy is the person that considers the poor, the Lord will deliver him in the day of evil* (Ps. 41:1)."[7]

In the above text there are two techniques in the art of honorable deception in the giving of *Tzedakah*, one was the "loan" and the other was the "gift." The Rabbis debated among themselves as to whether the donee should first be approached in terms of a loan or of a gift.

> "Our Rabbis taught: [If a man] has nothing and does not want to be supported [by *Tzedakah*] he should be given it [the money] as a loan and then it is given to him as a gift — according to R. Meir. And the Sages say: It is given to him as a gift and then it is given to him as a loan."[8]

The Rabbis were aware that some individuals have too much pride to accept "gifts;" by characterizing the transaction as a "loan" the donee may not be so reluctant to accept the indirect *Tzedakah*. Either alternative has the identical objective, namely, to give *Tzedakah* in an indirect manner so as not to embarrass the recipient.

Another ingenious form of honorable deception in the practice of *Tzedakah* is illuminated in the following story:

> "R. Shimᶜon b. Lakish went to Bozrah. There [he found] a man called Abba Yudan the Deceiver; not that he was, Heaven forbid, a dishonest man, but rather because he was cunning in *mitzvot*; for after all people had contributed, he contributed as much as all of them put together. R. Shimᶜon b. Lakish took him and gave him a seat next to himself. The verse, *A man's gift makes room for him, and brings him before great men* (Prov. 18:16) was applied to [Abba Yudan the Deceiver]."[9]

---

[7] *Vayikra Rabbah* 34:1; see also *Midrash* Tehilim 41:3.

[8] *Babylonian Talmud*, Ketubbot 67b.

[9] *Vayikra Rabbah* 5:4.

The trick of Abba Yudan in the above story was that while others were contributing *Tzedakah*, Abba Yudan refrained. The others were concerned that without the financial contributions of Abba Yudan the *Tzedakah* fund would be insufficient. Consequently, they gave more than they otherwise would have done to make up for Abba's deficiency. Then, after all the others had given to their absolute limit, Abba Yudan would match the entire sum. The text is unclear as to whether he would give his *Tzedakah* secretly. However, he probably could not have performed the above trick too many times in public while still retaining the title "Abba Yudan the Deceiver."

CHAPTER EIGHT: RULES AFFECTING THE DONOR OF *TZEDAKAH*

In the realm of *Tzedakah* certain expectations, obligations and restrictions were applicable to the donor. The most significant expectation that was placed upon the donor was that the *Tzedakah* given to the donee was suitable for his particular, unique needs. For example, if a family was in danger of starvation, giving them clothing would not be an appropriate expression of *Tzedakah.* It was incumbent upon the donor to investigate the circumstances of the prospective donee to determine what were his paramount needs. Of course, in an obvious or in an urgent situation one should dispense with the necessity of a careful investigation. In short, one should give wisely and with sensitivity.

The duty of the donor to satisfy the particular needs of each donee is illustrated by the rabbinic commentary to the following verse: *For the poor shall never cease out of the land; therefore I command you, saying: You shall open your hand wide unto your brother, to your poor and to your needy* (Deut. 15:11). The Rabbis were curious as to why three categories were listed in the above verse. Their explanation: "Who is worthy of bread is given bread, who is worthy of an *ʿisa* [a certain amount of flour] is given an *ʿisa*, who is worthy of a coin, is given a coin, who is worthy to be fed in his mouth, is fed in his mouth."[1]

Another biblical passage in the same chapter also was utilized by the Rabbis to discuss the obligations of the donor to meet the needs of the donee: *If there be among you a needy man, one of your brothers, within any of your gates, in your land which the Lord your God gives you, you shall not harden your heart, nor shut your hand from your needy brother; but you shall surely open your hand unto him, and shall surely lend him suffi-*

[1] *Sifré Deut.*118.

cient for his need in that which he wants (Deut. 15:7–8). The Rabbis analyzed this verse to determine how they should implement *Tzedakah.*

For example, if an orphan who was reliant upon *Tzedakah* expressed a desire to marry, the community should respond by 1) renting a house for him, 2) preparing a bed for him, 3) supplying him with household furnishings and 4) finding him a wife for marriage. "For it is written, *Sufficient for his need in that which he wants* (Deut. 15:8). *Sufficient for his need* refers to a bed and a table; *He* refers to a wife, for it is written: *And the Lord God said: It is not good that the man should be alone; I will make him a help mate for him* (Gen. 2:18)."[2]

The issue arises in respect to the above text, What does the word "sufficient" mean? What is the extent of the obligation of the donor to satisfy the requirement? "Our Rabbis taught: *Sufficient for his need* (Deut. 15:8) — you are commanded to support him, but you are not commanded to make him rich. *In that which he wants* (*ibid.*) — even a riding horse and a slave to run before him. It was told about Hillel the Elder that he bought a horse for a poor person from a good family, a riding-horse and a slave to run before him. Once he did not find a slave to run before him, so he ran before him for three miles."[3]

Thus the Rabbis required the donor to be cognizant of the economic circumstances of the donee before his recent misfortune drastically reduced his standard of living. It was the rabbinic objective that, if possible, the donor should assist the recipient in matching his previous standard of living. Otherwise, it would be too humiliating for a formerly wealthy individual to live as a beggar. This obligation sometimes fell upon an entire community. A small town in the Upper Galilee bought meat every day for a poor man who was from a good family. The meat was fowl and was quite an expense for the community. Nevertheless, it was perceived as a communal responsibility to enable this previously prosperous individual to live with some semblance of dignity.[4]

Another example of this expectation placed upon the donor:

---

[2] *Babylonian Talmud*, Ketubbot 67b.

[3] *Ibid.*

[4] *Ibid.*

> "A man once came to Rava. He said, What do you eat for meals? He said, Of fat chicken and old wine. He said, Do you not think of the burden upon the community? He said, Do I eat of theirs? I eat of the All-Merciful, for we have learnt: *The eyes of all wait for You, and You give them their food in its season* (Ps. 145:15). Thus, since it is not said "in their season" but "in his season," it teaches that the Holy One, blessed be He, provides for every individual his food in accordance with his own habits. In the meantime Rava's sister who had not seen him for thirteen years had come and brought him a fat chicken and old wine. He said, What a coincidence! And he said to him, I humble myself, come and eat."[5]

In addition to the prior economic circumstances of the recipient it is imperative to consider the present situation of the donee. Is he/she in transit? Is it *Shabbat*? For how long will the donee be in town? The rabbinic response:

> "But surely we have learnt: One does not give less than a loaf [sufficient for two meals] ... to a poor person travelling from place to place. If necessary, s/he must be supported when spending the night; while if s/he spends *Shabbat*, s/he must be given food for three meals ... For example, if s/he has one meal with her/him, we say to her/him, Eat that which you have with you. And when s/he leaves, shall s/he depart empty-handed? [No!] We provide her/him with a meal. What is meant by supporting someone for the night? R. Papa said: A bed and a pillow."[6]

From the above examples, it is evident that it was incumbent upon the donor to carefully determine how to best serve the particular needs of the prospective donee. Merely giving *Tzedakah* was not sufficient, one should give wisely. This would include giving the proper amount in an appropriate manner. This responsibility in respect to *Tzedakah* was commented upon by R. Yonah who said: "It is not written 'Happy is the one, who gives to the poor,' but

---

[5] *Ibid.*

[6] *Babylonian Talmud*, Shabbat 118a.

rather, *Happy is the one who considers [maskil] the poor* (Ps. 41:2) — which means, consider how to benefit him."[7] According to R. Yonah, *maskil* in the above verse indicates that the donor is required to use his insight when giving *Tzedakah*.

An additional obligation imposed upon the donor was that s/he give *Tzedakah* in a humble manner. If s/he was patronizing or condescending, s/he would probably humiliate the donee. This would be a terrible injustice. Humility was highly valued in the context of giving *Tzedakah* as set forth in the following passage.

> "Teach the members of your house humility. For when one is humble and the members of one's household are humble, if a poor person comes and stands in the doorway of the master of the house and inquires of them, Is your father within? They answer, Yes, come in, enter. Even before s/he has entered, a table is set for him/her. When s/he enters and eats and drinks and offers a blessing up to Heaven, great delight of spirit is given to the master of the house. But when one is not humble and the members of her/his household are impatient, if a poor person comes and stands in the doorway and inquires of them, Is your father within? They answer, No! and rebuke him/her and drive him/her off in anger."[8]

Thus it can be seen that the Rabbis greatly esteemed the attribute of humility and considered this attitude to be obligatory upon the donor of *Tzedakah*. Besides the above expectations and obligations placed upon the donor, there is a basic restriction: the donor must limit the amount of *Tzedakah* so that s/he her/himself does not create the possibility that s/he will be in need of *Tzedakah*. As demonstrated in chapter three, there were overly generous contributors of *Tzedakah* who in their zeal impoverished their own families. A mathematical limit had to be set so that one would have a guideline as to the extent of one's obligation. The Rabbis debated whether that limit should be a tenth of one's wealth or a fifth.

---

[7] *Vayikra Rabbah* 34:1; parallel *Talmud Yerushalmi*, Pe'ah 8:8.

[8] *Avot de Rabbi Natan* 7, version a, Schechter edition.

> "R. El'ai stated: It was decided at Usha that if a person wished to spend liberally s/he should not spend more than a fifth. So it was also taught: If a person desires to spend liberally [for *Tzedakah*] s/he should not spend more than a fifth [of his/her wealth], because s/he might her/himself come to be in need [of *Tzedakah*] from people … Where [is this found in Scripture]? *And of all that you shall give me I will surely give the tenth unto You* (Gen. 28:22). But the second tenth, surely, is not like the first one? — R. Ashi replied: I will … give a tenth of it [implies I will give] the second tenth like the first tenth."[9]

If one examines the above verse in Hebrew, one will note that the verb "to give a tenth" is repeated. The Rabbis contended that since the verb is repeated that indicated one could give as much as two-tenths or one fifth of one's wealth for *Tzedakah*.

However, there was an exception to the above maximum of one fifth of one's wealth. If the donor was dying there would no longer be the possibility of his jeopardizing his own financial future. Consequently, there is the "deathbed exception." "When Mar 'Ukba's soul was about to depart he said, Bring me the *Tzedakah* account. When he found that 7,000 *siyan* [gold] *denari* were entered on his account, he said, The provisions are poor and the road is long. And he arose and distributed half of his wealth. But how could this be? Has not R. El'ai said, It was decided at Usha that if a person wished to spend liberally s/he should not spend more than a fifth? This refers only to a person's lifetime, since s/he might become impoverished, but after death this does not matter."[10]

---

[9] *Babylonian Talmud*, Ketubbot 50a.
[10] *Babylonian Talmud*, Ketubbot 67b.

CHAPTER NINE: ALMS COLLECTORS

It soon became apparent that every needy donee could not readily find an available and willing donor to assist the donee in his/her particular circumstances. In order for the system of *Tzedakah* to function within a community there had to be some individuals who acted as liaisons between the donors and the donees. These individuals, known as alms collectors, acted in a dual capacity; they both collected and distributed *Tzedakah*. They had a difficult and demanding position within the community. In some respects the role of collecting *Tzedakah* was not as difficult as distributing *Tzedakah*. "R. Yose said: May my lot be of those who collect *Tzedakah*, but not of those who distribute *Tzedakah*."[1]

What concerned R. Yose was that in the role of collecting *Tzedakah* one could act with impartiality. Everyone was obligated to give and one generally did not have to engage in fine moral distinctions in respect to accepting their contributions. However, moral dilemmas were presented in the act of distribution. There usually was not sufficient *Tzedakah* to meet the needs of the poor. One had to select certain individuals to receive *Tzedakah* and reject others. One had to apportion the *Tzedakah* in a fair and equitable manner without permitting one's personal preferences to interfere with the demands of justice.

Alms collectors were generally esteemed within the community. They were perceived by some Rabbis as providing moral and spiritual leadership to the community. This is illustrated by the comment on the following verse: *And they that lead the many to right-*

---

[1] *Babylonian Talmud*, Shabbat 118b.

eousness will be like the stars for ever and ever (Dan. 12:3). These are the *Tzedakah* collectors."[2]

One measure of community esteem and the status of a profession is the willingness of parents to allow their children to marry members of that profession. "All whose fathers are known to have held office as public officers or alms collectors may marry into the priestly class and none need trace their descent."[3] To marry into the priestly class was to gain entry into the highest stratum of society.[4] Furthermore, one did not have to go through the difficulty of providing one's family genealogy.

Within the typical Jewish community there was a hierarchy of values as demonstrated by the priorities of suitable spouses for one's sons. Alms collectors were within the hierarchy but certainly not at the top. "Our Rabbis taught: Let a man always sell all he has and marry the daughter of a scholar. If he does not find the daughter of a scholar, let him marry the daughter of the honorable men of the generation [probably the civic leaders of the Jewish community]. If he does not find the daughter of the honorable men of the generation, let him marry the daughter of the head of the synagogue. If he does not find the daughter of the head of a synagogue, let him marry the daughter of a *Tzedakah* treasurer. If he does not find the daughter of a *Tzedakah* treasurer, let him marry the daughter of an elementary school-teacher, but let him not marry the daughter of an *ʿam ha-aretz* [an ignorant, illiterate person] ..."[5]

One reason that alms collectors were not universally popular was that they had the unpleasant task of quarrelling with the members of the community who did not pay their share of compulsory *Tzedakah*. This was the rabbinic explanation of why the *Mishnah* raised the issue of whether alms collectors may marry into the priesthood.[6]

---

[2] *Babylonian Talmud*, Bava Batra 8b.

[3] *Mishnah*, Kiddushin 4:5.

[4] Lee I. Levine, *The Rabbinic Class of Roman Palestine in Late Antiquity* (Jerusalem: Yad Yitzḥak Ben-Zvi Publications, 1989).

[5] *Babylonian Talmud*, Pesaḥim 49b.

[6] *Babylonian Talmud*, Kiddushin 76b.

Alms collectors had to be concerned with *marit ʿayin*, their appearance to others within the community. Their conduct had to be above suspicion; they could not give the appearance that they possibly may be misappropriating the *Tzedakah* fund which they collected. The Rabbis established certain standards of conduct to assure that the alms collectors would not be compromised.

> "Our Rabbis taught: The collectors of *Tzedakah* are not permitted to separate from one another, but one may [temporarily] separate himself [in order to collect] at the gate while [the other collects] at a shop. If one of them finds money in the market, he should not put it in his purse but into the *kupah* and when he comes home he should take it out. In the same way, if one of them has lent a person a *minah* and s/he pays him in the market, he should not put the money into his own purse but into the *kupah* and take it out again when he comes home … If the stewards of the *tamḥui* still have food and no poor to whom to distribute it, they may sell it to others but not to themselves. In counting out the money collected for *Tzedakah*, they should not count the coins two at a time, but only one at a time [people may think that they are counting one coin for every two received]."[7]

The Rabbis were aware that the system of *Tzedakah* within the community was dependent upon the assumption that the alms collectors were collecting and distributing the *Tzedakah* funds in an honorable manner. The entire structure could collapse if that assumption was undermined by inappropriate or suspicious conduct on the part of the alms collectors.

Furthermore, the Rabbis enacted certain procedural rules as to the mechanics of *Tzedakah* collection and distribution. "Our Rabbis taught: The *Tzedakah* fund is collected by two persons and distributed by three. It is collected by two, because any office conferring authority over the community must be filled by at least two [persons]. It must be distributed by three, on the analogy of money cases [which are adjudicated by a *Beit Din* comprised of three judg-

---

[7] *Babylonian Talmud*, Bava Batra 8b; a similar passage is found in *Babylonian Talmud*, Pesaḥim 13a.

es]. Food for the *tamḥui* is for all visitors, the *kupah* is for the poor of the community."[8]

The reason why *Tzedakah* funds must be distributed by three individuals is that like a *Beit Din* the collector may have to adjudicate the allocation of *Tzedakah* among competing claimants. Food is collected by three and distributed by three since the food is dispersed immediately. Any delay could result in spoilage of the perishable food.

Ultimately the system of *Tzedakah* collection was dependent upon the integrity of the individual alms collector. A donor should be careful that he give his *Tzedakah* to an alms collector of integrity. "A person should not put a *perutah* into the *kupah* unless it is under the supervision of a person like R. Ḥanina b. Teradion" [who was known to be reliable].[9]

A great deal of discretion was placed in the hands of the alms collectors. One issue confronted by them was whether the funds collected should be dispersed for the benefit of the inhabitants of the local community or whether the funds could be given to the poor from other communities. Should the alms collectors have two purses, one for each purpose? Should conditions be placed upon the alms collectors to limit their options? R. Ashi reacted negatively to this idea and stated: "I do not need to have conditions, since whoever comes [to give me money for *Tzedakah*] relies upon my judgment, and leaves it to me to give to whom I wish."[10]

Given this great amount of trust that was placed in the alms collectors the Rabbis did not require them to provide an accounting of the dispersal of the funds. The Rabbis could not find a biblical text directly supporting this position; however, they did cite the following as a partial justification. *They reckoned not with the men into whose hand they delivered the money, to give to them that did the work, for they dealt faithfully* (2 Kgs. 12:16).[11]

Tzedakah funds would on occasion be collected for a particular purpose. It was the responsibility of each alms collector to hon-

---

[8] *Ibid.*

[9] *Babylonian Talmud*, Bava Batra 10b; parallel *Kallah Rabbati* 51a–b.

[10] *Babylonian Talmud*, Bava Batra 9a.

[11] *Ibid.*

or the original intent of the donor. For example, R. Yose b. Kismal mistakenly confused the *Purim*-money for ordinary *Tzedakah* funds. To correct his error he gave his own funds to the poor at *Purim*, since he had already distributed the money that he had accepted for this purpose.[12]

In an era in which men made all significant financial decisions, women were not deemed competent to make substantial contributions of *Tzedakah*. Consequently, the alms collectors were limited to accepting only small donations from women. "Small donations" is a term dependent upon the relative wealth of the women.

> "Ravina came once to the city of Maḥuza. The housewives of Maḥuza came and threw before him chains and bracelets, which he accepted from them [for *Tzedakah*]. Said Rabbah Tosfa'ah to Ravina: Was it not taught: Alms collectors may accept from them small donations but not large amounts? He, said to him: These things are considered with the people of Maḥuza as small amounts."[13]

Alms collectors were capable of pressing people to give *Tzedakah* beyond their limits. If they forcibly demanded contributions in an amount in excess of what the donors could reasonably afford, the alms collectors themselves were inviting divine retribution: *And I will punish all that oppress them* (Jer. 30:20), "even collectors of *Tzedakah* …"[14]

One aspect of the genius of the rabbinic mind was its ingenious capacity to make fine distinctions. The above potential punishment for *Tzedakah* collectors was too sweeping for some Rabbis and thus they modified the statement. The qualification set forth below demonstrates the unique value that the study of Torah had within the Jewish community.

> "R. Berekhia and R. Ḥiya, his father, opened their discourse in the name of R. Yose bar Nehorai: It is written, *I will punish all*

---

[12] *Babylonian Talmud*, ʿAvodah Zarah 17b; similar passage *Kallah Rabbati* 52b.

[13] *Babylonian Talmud*, Bava Kama 119a.

[14] *Vayikra Rabbah* 30:1.

that oppress (Jer. 30:20), [this applies] even to collectors of *Tzedakah*. But it does not apply to those who collect money in behalf of teachers of Mishnah and the teachers of Bible, payment which the teachers of Mishnah and the teachers of Bible merit because they do not labor at some other employment in their own behalf. As to compensation for teaching even one word in the Torah, for such teaching no human being can give adequate compensation."[15]

[15] *Pesikta de Rav Kahana* 28, p. 178a, Buber edition.

CHAPTER TEN: THE PRIORITIES IN GIVING *TZEDAKAH*

Prior to any discussion of the priorities in giving *Tzedakah* it should be noted that no consistent hierarchy can be drawn from the scattered rabbinic sources that mention this topic. Different texts provide different lists of priorities. Nevertheless, these few rabbinic texts were later utilized by the codifiers of Jewish law as proof-texts for their elaborate codes listing a hierarchy of *Tzedakah*.[1]

Before commencing with any rabbinic sources as to how one should allocate *Tzedakah*, we must first confront the question: Suppose one does not have anything to give? Any list of priorities in giving *Tzedakah* assumes that one is in a position to distribute some wealth and furthermore, that one needs to make a choice in regard to this distribution. This assumption may not be valid for those individuals who are not in a position to give. One applicable biblical verse is *And if you draw out your soul to the hungry, and satisfy the afflicted soul; then shall your light rise in darkness, and your gloom be as the noonday* (Isa. 58:10). Relying on this verse, "R. Levi said, if you have nothing to give him, console him with words, speak to him: My soul goes forth to you, for I have nothing to give to you."[2] Thus even if one has nothing to give one should devote one's efforts to

---

[1] Maimonides, *Mishneh Torah*, Hilkhot matenot ʿaniyim. See generally: Abraham Cronbach, "The Gradations of Benevolence," *Hebrew Union College Annual* 16 (1941), 163–86, and Aaron Rosenberg, *A Translation of the "Laws of Tzedakah" in the Arba-ah Turim by Jacob Ben Asher and a Comparison Between Treatment of the Laws of Tzedakah in the Mishneh Torah, the Arba-ah Turim, and the Shulchan Aruch* (Rabbinic Thesis, Hebrew Union College-Jewish Institute of Religion, Cincinnati, 1974).

[2] *Vayikra Rabbah* 34:15.

comforting the soul of the supplicant for *Tzedakah*. Words of kindness, warmth and empathy may do more to raise the spirits of the afflicted soul than a few meager coins. Nevertheless, the above passage is inconsistent with *Babylonian Talmud*, Gittin 7b, which has the statement of Mar Zutra that "Even a poor person who himself/herself subsists on *Tzedakah* should give *Tzedakah*" (see chapter five).

Assuming one has something of substance to give, how should it be dispersed? One rabbinic response is that we are obligated to honor God first with any substance that we may have. This is from the verse, *Honor the Lord with your substance, And with the first-fruits of all your increase* (Prov. 3:9).

> "How is one to honor Him with one's substance? One sets aside gleanings, the over-looked sheaves and *pe'ah*, the first tithe, the second tithe and the *ḥallah* [the priest's share of dough]. One makes a *shofar*, a *sukkah* and a *lulav*; one feeds the hungry and gives drink to the thirsty and clothes the naked. If you have substance, you are obliged to do all of these, but if you are engaged in honoring your father and your mother, what is written? *Honor your father and your mother* (Exod. 20:12). Even if you have to walk around [and beg] at doorways."[3]

The above passage lists a variety of obligations assuming that one has the substance to comply with these *mitzvot*. It concurs with the text cited above that one who is without "substance" is relieved from the responsibility of giving *Tzedakah*. The one exception to this rule is that of honoring one's parents. According to this text, one has no excuse if one's parents are in want. Even if one has nothing, one must literally beg from door to door in order to give something of substance to one's parents.

Parents are given first priority in regard to allocation of *Tzedakah* in various rabbinic texts. An example is the following commentary on this biblical verse: *Is it not to deal your bread to the hungry, and that you bring the poor that are cast out to your house? When you see the naked, that you cover him, And that you hide not yourself from your own flesh?* (Isa. 58:7).

---

[3] *Pesikta Rabbati* 23/24:9, Ulmer ed.

> "So, if a person has many provisions in her/his house and wishes to do *Tzedakah*, where should s/he start? First, s/he should support her/his father and her/his mother. If s/he has something left, s/he should support the people in her/his neighborhood. Next, if s/he has something left, s/he should support the people on his street. And finally, s/he should provide *Tzedakah* to Israel."[4]

The above text describes a concentric circle of obligations. At the center, of primary responsibility, is the support of one's parents. At the periphery are the people of Israel. The primary obligation of providing for one's parents is further illustrated by the following text. Again the biblical referent is Isa. 58:7: *When you see the naked, that you cover him.*

> "When the Holy One, may His great name be blessed forever and ever!, saw Adam naked, He did not wait an hour but clothed him at once, as it is said, *And the Lord God made for Adam and for his wife* [*garments of skin, and clothed them*] (Gen. 3:21). Similarly, a person seeing his/her father and his/her mother standing in shabby garments. If s/he himself/herself wears clothing worth five *minah*, s/he should clothe his/her father and her/his mother in ten *minah's* worth, if s/he wears ten *minah's* worth, s/he should clothe her/his father and her/his mother in fifteen *minah's* worth. Her/his diminution is praise for them."[5]

Not only is one initially responsible to support one's parents, but at least in regard to clothing one should expend an even greater sum upon them than upon oneself.

Interestingly, the family diagram does not extend vertically in both directions. Although one appears to have the definite obligation of giving *Tzedkah* to one's parents, there are rabbinic passages that indicate that one is relieved of the responsibility of supporting one's children. This is consistent with the discussion in chapter two which indicates that one is not absolutely required to support one's

---

[4] *Seder Eliyahu Rabbah* 27, p. 135, Friedmann edition.

[5] *Ibid.*, p. 136.

children beyond a certain age. The exception is that a wealthy individual may be compelled to give *Tzedakah* to his children. Despite the known humiliation of having one's children accepting *Tzedakah*, there are rabbinic passages contending that one should have other priorities.

The Rabbis state that God Himself explained this verse: *The spirit of person is the lamp of the Lord* (Prov. 20:27).

> "The Holy One, blessed be He, said: Let My lamp be in your hand and your lamp in My hand, [i.e., keep My Torah and I will keep your soul in safety.] What is the lamp of God? The Torah, as it says, *For the mitzvah is a lamp, and the teaching is a light* (Prov. 6:23). What is *the mitzvah is a lamp*? Because everybody who performs a *mitzvah* is as if s/he has kindled a light before the Holy One, blessed be He, and if s/he has kindled a light before the Holy One, blessed be He, and as if s/he had revived his/her own soul, which is called a light, for it says, *The spirit of person is the lamp of the Lord* (Prov. 20:27). What is *the teaching is a light* (Prov. 6:23)? Because it often happens that when one is eager to fulfill a *mitzvah*, her/his Evil Inclination within her/him says to her/him: Why do you want to perform this *mitzvah* and diminish your wealth? Instead of giving away to others, give it to your own children. But the Good Inclination says to her/him: Give according to the *mitzvah*; for see what is written: *For the mitzvah is a lamp* (*ibid.*); just as the light of the lamp is undiminished even if a million wax and tallow candles are kindled from it, so will s/he who gives towards the fulfillment of any *mitzvah* not suffer a diminution of her/his possessions. Therefore, *For the mitzvah is a lamp, and the teaching is a light* (*ibid.*)."[6]

The intriguing portion of the above passage is that it is the Evil Inclination that tells the potential donor to give her/his wealth to her/his children; it is the Good Inclination that says to distribute it to others. The rabbinic justification was the belief that even if one distributed wealth outside the family, one's total wealth will ultimately not be decreased by this generosity. One relies upon God to

---

[6] *Shemot Rabbah* 36:3.

make up the difference as well as to take care of one's children. This reliance upon God to take care of one's children after they have reached maturity is demonstrated in the following text.

> "R. Meir was a good scribe and had three *sela'* every *Shabbat*: He spent one *sela'* on food and drink, another on clothing, and the third on the support of rabbinical scholars. His disciples asked him, What are you doing for your children? He said, If they are righteous, then it will be as David said, *Yet have I not seen the righteous forsaken, nor his seed begging bread* (Ps. 37:25). If they are not righteous, why should I leave my possessions to the enemies of the Omnipresent? Therefore Solomon said, *And who knows whether he will be a wise person or a fool* (Eccl. 2:19)?"[7]

R. Meir believed that if his children were righteous God would provide for them and thus he should not give them *Tzedakah*. If they were not righteous, God would not give his children sustenance, but then the attitude of R. Meir was that he should not support his children if they were not righteous.

In connection with priorities, it should be understood that the economic circumstances of the recipient are not the only consideration of how to allocate *Tzedakah*. There are social and emotional needs as well, as these may influence the priorities of distribution of *Tzedakah*. For example,

> "Our Rabbis taught: If an orphan boy and an orphan girl applied for support, the girl orphan is to be supported first and the boy orphan afterwards because it is the way of a man to go [begging] on doorways but it is not the way of a woman to do so. If an orphan boy and an orphan girl applied for marriage, they marry the girl first and the boy orphan is married afterwards, because the shame of a woman is greater than that of a man."[8]

Here the concept of being eligible for *Tzedakah* is expanded beyond economic deprivation. One can incur a sense of shame and a con-

---

[7] *Kohelet Rabbah* 2:1, 17.

[8] *Babylonian Talmud*, Ketubbot 67a–67b.

current loss of self-esteem by not being married. In the case of a woman who had reached marriageable age, this could result in an acute sense of *bushah* or embarrassment. The Rabbis were under the impression that her embarrassment of not being able to marry would be greater than that of the male orphan. Consequently, the resources of the community, including its economic resources should first be assigned to her marriage.

Another consideration of the Rabbis in determining priorities was the purpose of the *Tzedakah* and the circumstances under which it was given. Did the *Tzedakah* have the potential to bring about a permanent transformation in the status of the donee? These questions were implicitly raised in the following two textual passages: "R. Abba said [in the name] of R. Shimʿon b. Lakish: One who lends [money] is greater than one who does *Tzedakah*; and he who forms a partnership is greater than all."[9] A similar point of view is expressed in this passage: "Upon her/him who gives alms shall come a blessing. But greater than s/he is the lender, and highest of all is s/he who shares half of the profit."[10]

Both texts state that lending money is a greater deed than giving *Tzedakah* unconditionally. How could this be? We may speculate that a loan creates for the donee a psychological obligation as well as a legal one. This psychological obligation may be so strong as to influence the recipient to find a way to become self-sufficient in order to repay the loan. In addition, her/his sense of dignity is not as adversely affected if s/he believes that s/he is obtaining a loan rather than a gift. (Refer to chapter seven).

In any event, the greatest method of helping another is enabling the other person to gain self-sufficiency. This is implicit in the concept of partnership of sharing profits. The money is utilized in such a manner that income is created and shared between the two individuals. The income that is produced is sufficient to enable the "donee" to escape from dependence upon others and her/his self-esteem is immeasurably enhanced. Maimonides later utilized these two sources in his formulation of his famous Ladder of *Tzedakah* with its eight rungs.

---

[9] *Babylonian Talmud*, Shabbat 63a.

[10] *Avot de Rabbi Natan*, 41, version a, p. 131, Schechter edition.

Maimonides lists Eight Levels of Giving (*Mishneh Torah*, Hilkhot matenot ʿaniyim, 10:7–14):

1. Giving an interest-free loan to a person in need; forming a partnership with a person in need; giving a grant to a person in need; finding a job for a person in need; so long as that loan, grant, partnership, or job results in the person no longer living by relying upon others.
2. Giving *Tzedakah* anonymously to an unknown recipient via a person (or public fund) which is trustworthy, wise, and can perform acts of *Tzedakah* with your money in a most impeccable fashion.
3. Giving *Tzedakah* anonymously to a known recipient.
4. Giving *Tzedakah* publicly to an unknown recipient.
5. Giving *Tzedakah* before being asked.
6. Giving adequately after being asked.
7. Giving willingly, but inadequately.
8. Giving in sadness (giving out of pity or giving unwillingly).

Although the final text for this chapter does not deal with *Tzedakah* directly, it can be used for purposes of comparison since it deals with priorities in lending money. The commentary is on the verse: *If you lend money to any of My people, even to the poor with you, you shall not be to him as a creditor; neither shall you lay upon him interest* (Exod. 22:24). The particular words analyzed are *To any of My people.*

> "If an Israelite and a Gentile stand before you to borrow, *any of My people* should be given preference; if it be a poor person and a rich man, the poor person should be given preference; if it be your own poor [your relatives] and the poor of your city, your own poor should be given preference over the poor of your city; if it be the poor of your city and the poor of another city, the poor of your city should be given preference, for it is said: *Even to the poor with you.*"[11]

---

[11] *Mekilta De-Rabbi Ishmael*, Lauterbach edition (Philadelphia: The Jewish Publication Society of America, 1976), vol. 3, p. 148; parallel *Babylonian Talmud*, Bava Metzia 71a.

The theme of the above passage is that one's loyalties should consistently be extended to those who are nearest and closest.

CHAPTER ELEVEN: VOWS AND *TZEDAKAH*

In this discussion it is first necessary to distinguish between the two legal concepts of "oath" and "vow." Under Talmudic law an oath was a method of judicial proof and was utilized in civil cases. In the event that there was insufficient evidence in the civil litigation one of the parties would be permitted to take an "oath" in order to rebut or to confirm previous testimony. Generally speaking, non-judicial oaths were deemed "vows."[1]

Vows are promises made under religious sanction. Under Talmudic law there are two principal kinds of vows: "(1) A voluntary promise to bring a sacrifice which he who makes the vow is not otherwise in duty bound to bring; or a promise to give a certain sum to purposes of common charity or education … (2) The second chief kind of vow consists in promises made to abstain from the enjoyment of certain things …"[2]

This chapter will focus upon the first type of vows of making a promise to give *Tzedakah*. This type of vow falls under the category of "dedication" (*nidrei hekdesh*). One legal issue that is raised by *nidrei hekdesh* is what is the liability of the person who makes the vow if the item that has been promised is lost after the vow has been made.

> "When he who promises points toward the object which he intends to give, and says, 'This I dedicate to such and such a holy charitable cause,' then he is not bound to replace the thing if it

[1] *Encyclopedia Judaica*, "Oath," vol. 12, 1295–1302; *The Jewish Encyclopedia*, "Oaths," vol. 9, 365–67. See Moshe Ulmer, *The Rabbinic Concept of Tsedakah* (Rabbinical Thesis; Hebrew Union College, Cincinnati, 1988), 107–108.

[2] *The Jewish Encyclopedia*, "Vows," vol. 12, 451–52.

> is lost … If, on the other hand he says, 'I promise such and such an object, or such and such a sum of money to be devoted to that purpose,' then he is bound to replace it if it becomes lost. The former kind of vows are called 'nedaba' (= 'gift'); the latter kind 'neder' ('promise')."[3]

The significance that the Rabbis attached to vows is indicated by their devoting an entire tractate in the *Talmud* to the subject. The tractate, *Nedarim*, analyzes the eleven chapters of the *Mishnah* dealing with vows.[4] The above tractate does not include the Nazirite vow to which a separate tractate is devoted, nor does it concentrate on "oaths," which are discussed in tractate *Shevu'ot*.

In the last tractate mentioned, *Shevu'ot*, there is a text demonstrating the point that one may not make an "oath" concerning *Tzedakah*, since one is already obligated to give *Tzedakah*. "[If] s/he said, I swear that I shall give so-and-so, or, I shall not give. What is meant by 'I shall give?' Shall we say, *Tzedakah* to the poor? S/he already stands adjured from Mount Sinai, for it is said, *You shall surely give* (Deut. 15:10) — it must therefore mean a gift to a rich man."[5] In the rabbinic frame of reference all *mitzvot* were given at Mount Sinai. All Jews of all generations were present in person or in spirit at this moment of revelation and are obligated to perform the commandments. One of these *mitzvot* was to give *Tzedakah* to the poor (Deut. 15:7–11). One cannot take an "oath" to fulfill a *mitzvah*. One is already under an obligation to perform the *mitzvah* and such an "oath" is a nullity. Consequently, in the above passage the Rabbis reasoned that the "Oath" applied to giving something to a rich man, for whom one is not under a divine commandment to provide support.

The concept of vows and *Tzedakah* was already briefly alluded to in chapter four. One of the penalties inflicted upon a community if a member did not honor his vows regarding *Tzedakah* was the withholding of rain. A parallel text speculates as to why there was famine during the kingdom of David. "There might be among you

---

[3] *Ibid.*

[4] *Encyclopaedia Judaica*, "Vows and Vowing," vol. 16, 227.

[5] *Babylonian Talmud*, Shevu'ot 25a.

men who subscribe to *Tzedakah* in public but do not give them, as it is written, *As vapors and wind without rain, so is he that boasts himself of a false gift* (Prov. 25:14)."[6] Both the wind and the braggart fail to deliver their "gift" as expected.

In some instances the community would not tolerate the situation in which a member failed to honor his commitment in respect to *Tzedakah*. The community justifiably relied upon the pledge of such an individual and could not permit an undesirable precedent to be established. The entire system of *Tzedakah* could be jeopardized if people did not keep their vows and thus, on occasion, the community would expropriate the property of those individuals who did not comply with their public vows.

> "And on account of four things is the property of householders given into the hands of the government: On account of those who retain in their possession bills which have been paid [with the intention of colleting upon them a second time]; on account of them who lend money on usury; on account of those who had the power to protect [against wrongdoing] and did not protest; and on account of those who publicly subscribe to *Tzedakah* and do not give."[7]

The Rabbis generally discouraged individuals from making vows, since the consequences were so serious. In both the biblical and rabbinic eras there was a strong belief in the power of the spoken word. One was strongly cautioned to weigh one's words carefully. This point of view is revealed in Eccl. 5:1–6. For example, Eccl. 5:5 states: *suffer not your mouth to bring your flesh into guilt, neither say you before the messenger, that it was an error; wherefore should God be angry at your voice, and destroy the work of your hands.* There is a rabbinic commentary on this verse.

> "R. Yehoshuʿa b. Levi interpreted the verse relating to those who undertake to subscribe to *Tzedakah* but do not pay. *Neither say you before the messenger* — that is the official [alms-collector], *that is was an error* — [saying] I am sorry {I cannot pay}. *Where-*

[6] *Babylonian Talmud*, Yevamot 78b.

[7] *Babylonian Talmud*, Sukkot 29a–b.

> *fore should God be angry at your voice* — at the voice with which you said [that you would give *Tzedakah*]. *And destroy the work of your hands* — on the few pious acts which are in the hands of that man, the Holy One, blessed be He, brings a curse and causes them to be lost to him."[8]

What was almost as harmful to the system of *Tzedakah* as the one who failed to keep her/his vow was the individual who delayed payment. A vow to pay *Tzedakah* had to be paid in a timely manner. The primary biblical proof-text for this Talmudic position is Deut. 23:22 which states: *When you shall vow a vow to the Lord your God, you shall not delay to pay it; for the Lord your God will surely require it of you; and it will be a sin in you.*

A vow of giving Tzedakah had to be paid promptly, even if the donor did not specify a fixed date at the time s/he made the vow. S/he could not delay indefinitely; otherwise, the vow became meaningless. Consequently, the Rabbis created a date for the vow to take effect, even if no such date was originally given. The Talmudic discussion focuses on the three pilgrimage festivals, *Pesaḥ*, *Shavuᶜot*, and *Sukkot*, as having the capacity to trigger the date that the vow comes into effect.

The following discussion includes vows concerning *Tzedakah* and other obligations in which the date of performance is at issue.

> "Our Rabbis taught: Those who are liable for a money valuation, for a valuation, for a *ḥerem* [something devoted], for consecrations, for sin-offerings, tithes, firstborn and tithe of cattle, paschal lamb, gleanings, forgotten sheaves and *pe'ah*, as soon as three festivals have elapsed transgress the *mitzvah* of *not delaying* (Deut. 23:22). R. Shimᶜon said: The three festivals must be in their order, with *Pesaḥ* first. R. Meir said: As soon as one festival has passed, s/he transgresses the *mitzvah* of *not delaying*. R. Eliᶜezer b. Yaᶜakov said; As soon as two festivals have lapsed, s/he transgresses the *mitzvah* of *not delaying*. R. Eleᶜazar b. R.

---

[8] *Kohelet Rabbah* 5:1; see also *Midrash Tehillim* 52:1.

> Shim'on said: As soon as *Shavu'ot* has passed, he transgresses the *mitzvah* of *not delaying*."[9]

As can be seen, there is a dispute among the Rabbis as to whether one, two or three festivals have to transpire before the obligation becomes immediately effective. The Talmudic argument continues and another biblical verse is analyzed, namely Deut. 23:24, *That which is gone out of your lips you shall observe and do; according as you have vowed freely unto the Lord your God, even that which you have promised with your mouth.*

Each phrase in the above verse is dissected by the Rabbis to different obligations. "Our Rabbis taught: *That which is gone out of your lips* (Deut. 23:24) — this is an affirmative *mitzvah. You shall observe* — this is a negative *mitzvah. And do* — this is a warning to the *Beit Din* to make you do. *According as you have vowed* — this is a vow. *To the Lord your God* — these are sin-offerings. *Freely* — this is a free-will-offering *in its literal meaning. Even that which you have promised* — these are the things sanctioned for the repair of the Temple. *With your mouth* — this is *Tzedakah*."[10]

Thus finally at the very conclusion of the verse in question the rabbinic interpretation of the three words, *with your mouth*, is that they apply to the *mitzvah* of *Tzedakah*. This leads to another Talmudic discussion in which the author contends that *Tzedakah* is a unique *mitzvah* that should be differentiated from other *mitzvot* and not dependent upon the passage of festivals.

With your mouth (Deut. 23:24), "this is *Tzedakah*. Rava said, For *Tzedakah* one becomes liable at once. What is the reason? Because the poor are waiting. Surely this is obvious? You might think that, as *Tzedakah* is mentioned in the passage dealing with offerings, [it need not be paid] until the three festivals have transpired, as [in the case of] offerings. We are therefore told this is not so. Only the other [offerings] were made by the All-Merciful dependent upon festivals, but this [*Tzedakah*] is not so, because the poor are waiting."[11]

---

[9] *Babylonian Talmud*, Rosh Hashanah 4a–b.

[10] *Ibid.*, 6a.

[11] *Ibid.*

The reasoning in the last passage distinguishes *Tzedakah* from the other *mitzvot* in question. If one did not immediately honor one's vow of *Tzedakah*, the poor, who rely upon *Tzedakah*, may die in the interim. (See chapter six).

Still another legal issue in regard to vows is whether one may use or exchange an item after one has already vowed that it will be given for *Tzedakah*. Does the one who still possesses the item have any ownership rights or has s/he lost all control over the item? For example, if one pledges or vows to give a coin or an amount equivalent to several coins to *Tzedakah*, is one permitted to exchange these coins after a vow has been made? "R. Naḥman said in the name of R. Avuha, If one says: This *sela'* is for *Tzedakah*, s/he is permitted to exchange it."[12] Thus one is not relieved of one's obligation to give a *sela'* but one does not have to give the identical *sela'* that s/he may have held in her/his hand at the time s/he made the vow. Since the coins were interchangeable and of equivalent value, one could retain the particular *sela'* that one held at the time of the vow and substitute another.

A distinction was further drawn between vows for *Tzedakah* and consecrations to the sanctuary. Something vowed for *Tzedakah* could still be used by the owner, at least temporarily, while in the case of consecration, one may not use the item after it has been consecrated, or set apart for holy use.[13] This practice contradicts the text above which states that *Tzedakah* immediately becomes due and payable upon the making of the vow since the "poor are waiting."

The next question raised is whether one may exchange the money pledged to *Tzedakah* after it had already been given to the alms collector. There are two diametrically opposed views on this, "Our Rabbis taught: If one said: This *sela'* shall be for *Tzedakah*, then before it has reached the hand of the *Tzedakah* treasurer, it is permitted to exchange it, but after it has come into the treasurer's hand, it is forbidden to exchange it. But it is not so, for R. Yannai borrowed and then paid it. — It is different with R. Yannai, for

---

[12] *Babylonian Talmud*, ʿArakhin 6a.

[13] *Ibid.*

what he did was acceptable to the poor. The more he delayed the more did he succeed in collecting and bringing in to them."[14]

If one takes literally the passage *You shall not delay it* (Deut. 23:22), the *Tzedakah* should be immediately distributed by the alms collector once he received the money that has been vowed. An exception to this rule was made in the case of R. Yannai who himself was a treasurer of *Tzedakah*. He apparently delayed the distribution of *Tzedakah* by borrowing from the funds collected. However, once he returned the funds he added a surplus to the original amount. Needless to say the idea of "borrowing funds" by the treasurer of *Tzedakah* could lead to embezzlement; however, this issue was not raised by the Rabbis. Again the system of *Tzedakah* was based upon the integrity of the alms collector.

---

[14] *Ibid.*, 6a–b.

CHAPTER TWELVE: MOTIVATION IN GIVING *TZEDAKAH*

The motivation of the donor at the time that s/he performed *Tzedakah* was not of major concern to the Rabbis. The manner in which *Tzedakah* was given and whether or not the *Tzedakah* met the particular needs of the recipient were of far greater significance. There are only a few references in rabbinic literature that refer to the state of mind of the donor. The statements are somewhat inconsistent. One text that is directly applicable to the subject matter of this chapter is as follows:

> "R. Yudah b. R. Shalom explained: In the same way as a person's food is determined for him from *Rosh Hashanah* so are his losses determined for him from *Rosh Hashanah*. If he is merited — *Deal your bread to the hungry* (Isa. 58:7) and if he is not merited then he will — *bring the poor that are outcast to his house* (*ibid.*). [The following] is about the sons of Raban Yoḥanan b. Zakai's sister. He [Raban Yoḥanan b. Zakai] saw in a dream that they would lose 700 *denari* in that year. He forced them to give *Tzedakah* until only seventeen *denari* were left. On *ʿErev Yom Kippur* the Emperor's house sent and seized them [the remaining *denari*]. Raban Yoḥanan b. Zakai said, Do not fear [that you will lose any more]; you had seventeen *denari* and these they have taken. They [his nephews] said to him, How did you know what was going to happen? He said: I saw it in a dream. They said, Why did you not tell us? He said, Because I wanted you to do a *mitzvah* for its own sake."[1]

[1] *Babylonian Talmud*, Bava Batra 10a.

In the above passage the nephew had given *Tzedakah* without an ulterior motive. Raban Yoḥanan b. Zakai was aware that all their money would be confiscated by the government. Apparently he became aware of this through a dream that occurred at the time of *Rosh Hashanah.* During the next ten days prior to *Yom Kippur* he convinced his nephew to give virtually all his money for the purpose of *Tzedakah.* If the nephew had advance notice that they would lose all their money at *ʿErev Yom Kippur,* they may have acted differently. In any event, this text is a rabbinic text that is concerned that *Tzedakah* be performed for its own sake.[2]

A more typical passage is one in which the donor is cognizant of some benefit at the time that he gives *Tzedakah.* For example,

> "R. Ḥiyya said to his wife, When a poor person comes, be quick to offer him/her bread, so that others may be quick to offer it to your children. She exclaimed, You curse them by suggesting that they may become beggars! A verse is written, he said, *because [biglal] that for this thing* (Deut. 15:10), whereby the School of R. Yishmaʾel taught: It is a wheel that revolves in the world. It was taught, R. Gamliel b. Rabbi said, *And he shall give you mercy, and have compassion upon you, and multiply you* (Deut. 13:18). He who is merciful to others, mercy is shown to her/him in Heaven, while s/he who is not merciful to others, mercy is not shown to her/him by Heaven."[3]

In the above text there is a *quid pro quo* mentality. The donor gives *Tzedakah* because he believes that his children will ultimately benefit from his actions. They will need *Tzedakah* themselves, since poverty is cyclical and will eventually affect one's family (see chapter two). The donor in this instance is resigned to the prospect that poverty will blight his children. However, by giving *Tzedakah* now he will ameliorate their future misfortune. The most succinct text which boldly justifies giving *Tzedakah* with an ulterior motive is the following: "It was taught: If one says, This *selaʾ* is for *Tzedakah* in

---

[2] A story is found in *Vayikra Rabbah* 34:12 which mentions *Tzedakah* and concludes with the same phrase of doing a *mitzvah* for its own sake.

[3] *Babylonian Talmud*, Shabbat 151b.

order that my children may live and that I may merit the future world, s/he is completely righteous."[4]

One's motivation is largely irrelevant; what is of paramount significance is that one performs *Tzedakah*. The above text is discussed by Abraham Cronbach:

> "Somewhat divergent is the thought based on Bava Batra 10b, that one is a full fledged *Tzadik* even though one says, 'I gave this coin in order that my children may live' or 'that I might enjoy the hereafter' ... One who is already a perfect *Tzadik* does not lose that rank by speaking thus. One who is not already a perfect *Tzadik* becomes such by the mere act of philanthropy. The motive may not be the most exalted. But charity is exalted. The poor have been helped."[5]

However, motivation is not completely irrelevant to the rabbinic mind. In the same passage as cited by Cronbach, a distinction is made between the state of mind of an Israelite and an idolater. Even if an idolater gives *Tzedakah*, he is not considered righteous because of his evil motives. One possible explanation of this troublesome passage is that regardless of what the Israelite states, he really is giving *Tzedakah* for its own sake. Nevertheless, the following text illustrates an ethnocentric perspective of a persecuted minority which was living in the Land of Israel under Roman rule.

> "Raban Yoḥanan b. Zakai said to his disciples: My sons, what is the meaning of the verse, *Tzedakah exalts a people, but the kindness of the nations is sin* (Prov. 14:34)? R. Eliᶜezer answered and said: *Tzedakah* exalts a people — this is Israel of which it is written, *Who is like Your people Israel one nation on the earth?* (2 Sam. 7:23) *But the kindness of the nations is sin* (Prov. 14:34), all the *Tzedakah* and kindness done by the nations and the idolaters is counted to them as sin, because they only do it to magnify themselves, as it says, *That they may offer sacrifices of sweet savor*

---

[4] *Babylonian Talmud*, Bava Batra 10b; parallel *Babylonian Talmud*, Pesaḥim 8a–b. See also *Babylonian Talmud*, Bava Batra 9b.

[5] Abraham Cronbach, "Meᶜil Zedakah — Second Article," *Hebrew Union College Annual* 12–13 (1937–1938), 635–96, 671.

> *unto God of heaven and pray for the life of the king and of his sons* (Ezra 6:10). But this is not complete *Tzedakah*, seeing that it has been taught: If a person says, I give this *sela'* for *Tzedakah* in order that my children may live and that I merit the future world, s/he is completely righteous. There is no contradiction, in the one case we speak of an Israelite, in the other of an idolater … because they only do it in order that their dominion may be prolonged … because they only do it to display haughtiness, and whoever displays haughtiness is cast into *Gehinom* … since they do it only to reproach us."[6]

Thus in the above passage the motive of the "idolater" in doing *Tzedakah* vitiates the act, while the motive of the "Israelite" does not affect the merit of the act. However, in the same text there is a mitigating sentence which attributes some benefit to the other nations of the world that perform *Tzedakah*. "As it has been taught: R. Yoḥanan b. Zakai said to them, Just as the sin-offering makes atonement for Israel, so *Tzedakah* makes atonement for the nations of the world."[7]

As stated in the introductory paragraph of this chapter, the texts in question simply do not present any discernible pattern in respect to motivation. The Hebrew word *kavanah* is not found in the above texts. The Rabbis were not directly concerned with the "intention" of the donor. The only references are to the "motivation" of the donor and these references have inconsistent conclusions as to the significance of this state of mind.

---

[6] *Babylonian Talmud*, Bava Batra 10b; see also *Babylonian Talmud*, Rosh Hashanah 4a.

[7] *Babylonian Talmud*, Bava Batra 10b.

CHAPTER THIRTEEN: *TZEDAKAH* IN RELATION TO OTHER *MITZVOT*

In comparing the *mitzvah* of *Tzedakah* to the other *mitzvot*, *Tzedakah* was often considered one of the most important *mitzvot* that could be performed. One explanation for this is that *Tzedakah* has the capacity to deliver a human being from death as stated in Prov. 10:2. This quality of *Tzedakah* gives it a special status among the *mitzvot*. The Rabbis have written in regard to *Tzedakah*: "And there is no drug as effective against death as *Tzedakah* … And the wise taught: Who preserves one soul of Israel it is as if s/he preserves a whole world."[1] As can be seen from chapter three, few *mitzvot* have the power of *Tzedakah*.

In order to emphasize the importance of a particular *mitzvah*, the Rabbis frequently characterize its performance as equivalent in merit to the performance of all other *mitzvot* combined. Since no one actually performs all 613 *mitzvot*, the Rabbis have created an alternative system in which the performance of certain *mitzvot* earns the same *kavod* (honor) in the eyes of God as if that individual had actually observed all the *mitzvot*. *Tzedakah* is one of the few *mitzvot* that has this special function. This viewpoint is expressed in the rabbinic comment on the verse *If you lend money to any of My people, even to the poor with you, you shall not be to him as a creditor; neither shall you lay upon him interest* (Exod. 22:24).

> "This is what is written, *He that puts not out his money on interest* (Ps. 15:5). Come and see: anyone who has riches and gives *Tzedakah* to the poor, and does not lend on interest is regarded as if s/he observed all the *mitzvot*, for it says, *One that puts not*

[1] *Seder Eliyahu Rabbah* 11, pp. 52–53, Friedmann edition.

out his money on interest, nor takes a bribe against the innocent. One that does these things shall never be moved (Ps. 15:5)."[2]

Nevertheless, *Tzedakah* is not always given the highest value among the *mitzvot*. The subsequent rabbinic interpretations pertaining to the value of *Tzedakah* are based upon a series of verses in Isaiah 58:

> (7) *Is it not to deal your bread to the hungry and bring the poor to your house who are cast out; when you see the naked, that you cover him, and not hide yourself from your own flesh?* (8) *Then your light shall break forth like the morning, your healing shall spring forth speedily, and your righteousness shall go before you; the glory of the* LORD *shall be your rear guard.* (9) *Then you shall call, and the* LORD *will answer; you shall cry, and He will say, 'Here I am.' If you take away the yoke from your midst, the pointing of the finger, and speaking wickedness,* (10) *and if you draw out your soul to the hungry, and satisfy the afflicted soul; then shall your light rise in darkness, and your gloom will be as noonday;* (11) *and the Lord will guide you continually; and satisfy your soul in drought and strengthen your bones; you shall be like a watered garden, and like a spring of water, whose waters do not fail.* (12) *And they that shall be of you shall build the old waste places, You shall raise up the foundations of many generations And you shall be called the Repairer of the Breach, the Restorer of streets to dwell in.* (Isa. 58:7–12)

The following text illustrates that there are actions that one may take that will provide greater comfort to the poor than the mere act of giving them *Tzedakah*.

> "R. Yitzḥak said, He who gives a *perutah* to a poor person obtains the blessings and s/he who comforts with words obtains eleven blessings. S/he who gives a *perutah* to a poor person contains six blessings, as it is written, *Is it not to deal your bread to the hungry and bring the poor to your house … when you see the naked* (Isa. 58:7).[3] He who comforts him with words obtains eleven blessings,[4] as it is written, *And if you draw out your soul to the hungry, And satisfy the afflicted soul; then shall your light rise in darkness,*

---

[2] *Shemot Rabbah* 31:4.

[3] The six blessings are found in Isa. 58:8–9.

[4] The eleven blessings are found in Isa. 58:10–12.

> *And your gloom will be as noonday; And the Lord will guide you continually; And satisfy your soul in drought … And they that shall be of you shall build the old waste places, You shall raise up the foundations of many generations* (Isa. 58:10–12)."[5]

The Rabbis chose to interpret the Bible literally, if it served their homiletical purpose. In the above texts the actions of *Tzedakah* are described in Isa. 58:7, namely, giving bread to the poor, bringing the poor into one's house, and clothing them. The six different rewards for this *mitzvah* are set forth immediately afterwards, Isa. 58:8–9. In Isa. 58:10 a different type of *mitzvah* is described, namely, to be compassionate and *to satisfy the afflicted soul.* After this conduct is described in the first half of Isa. 58:10, the Rabbis counted eleven separate blessings from the second half of Isa. 58:10 to the end of Isa. 58:12. These eleven blessings were the direct reward of the actions set forth in the first half of Isa. 58:10. The Rabbis interpreted this portion of the verse to mean to be compassionate with one's words to the hungry person and to give her/him some emotional comfort. They considered this a more difficult and a more valuable *mitzvah* than merely giving physical items to the poor. They justified their preference by interpreting Isa. 58:7–12 as stating that one received six blessings for the *mitzvah* of *Tzedakah* and eleven blessings for comforting the poor with words.

The actions described in Isa. 58:10, as interpreted in the above text, would fall under the category of *Gemilut Ḥasadim*. Generally, the Rabbis contended that *Gemilut Ḥasadim* was a more significant *mitzvah* than *Tzedakah*. Their reasoning is demonstrated in the following passage. "*Tzedakah* and *Gemilut Ḥasadim* are like all *mitzvot* in the Torah, only that *Tzedakah* applies to the living and *Gemilut Ḥasadim* to the dead, *Tzedakah* to the poor and *Gemilut Ḥasadim* to the poor and the rich, *Tzedakah* to money and *Gemilut Ḥasadim* to money and the body."[6]

Tzedakah can only be given to a living person; it is useless to a person who is already deceased. However, one can perform acts of *Gemilut Ḥasadim* on behalf of the dead. For example, the act of *ta-*

---

[5] *Babylonian Talmud*, Bava Batra 9b.

[6] *Tosefta*, Pe'ah 4, p. 60, Liebermann edition.

harah, the ritual washing of the corpse, is an act of *Gemilut Ḥasadim*. *Tzedakah* is only given to those in need, namely, the poor. One cannot give *Tzedakah* to a rich person since s/he does not have the need. However, one can perform an act of *Gemilut Ḥasadim* for a rich person. The act of *bikur ḥolim*, visiting the sick, can be done for a rich person as well as a poor person. *Tzedakah* requires that one gives wealth, usually money, to another person. For example, if a person is carrying a very heavy burden one could offer to share that burden. In doing so one is actually performing an act of *Gemilut Ḥasadim* with one's body.

A similar viewpoint of the superiority of *Gemilut Ḥasadim* over *Tzedakah* is found in the following text:

> "R. Eleᶜazar said, Greater is he who does *Tzedakah* than [he who offers] all the sacrifices, for it is said, *To do Tzedakah and justice is more acceptable to the Lord than sacrifice* (Prov. 21:3). R. Eleᶜazar said, *Gemilut Ḥasadim* is greater than *Tzedakah*, for it is said, *Sow yourselves according to your Tzedakah, but reap according to your Ḥesed* (Hos. 10:12);[7] if a person sows, it is doubtful, whether s/he will eat or not, but when a person reaps, s/he will certainly eat … Our Rabbis taught: In three respects is *Gemilut Ḥasadim* superior to *Tzedakah*. *Tzedakah* is done with one's money, but *Gemilut Ḥasadim* is done with one's person and one's money. *Tzedakah* can be given only to the poor, *Gemilut Ḥasadim* [can be given to] both the rich and the poor. *Tzedakah* can be given to the living only, *Gemilut Ḥasadim* can be done both to the living and to the dead."[8]

Gemilut Ḥasadim is acknowledged to be superior to *Tzedakah*, since it has more universal application. It is a more flexible *mitzvah* in that it is not dependent upon the dispersal of funds. Even a destitute person who is simply unable to give any *Tzedakah*, despite the caveat of *Babylonian Talmud*, Gittin 7b that a poor person who himself/herself receives *Tzedakah* should give *Tzedakah*, can still perform *Gemilut Ḥasadim*. Nevertheless, in the same passage as quoted above, R. Eleᶜazar declares the unique and valuable role of *Tzed-*

---

[7] *Ḥesed* refers to *Gemilut Ḥasadim*.

[8] *Babylonian Talmud*, Sukkah 49b.

akah. "He who does *Tzedakah* and justice is regarded as though he had filled all the world with kindness, for it is said, *he loves Tzedakah and justice; the earth is full of the loving-kindness of the Lord* (Ps. 33:5)."[9]

Earlier in the above text *Tzedakah* is considered to be a greater *mitzvah* than that of offering sacrifices. The superiority of *Tzedakah* over sacrifice is discussed in much greater detail in the following passage:

> "This is what Scripture says, *To do Tzedakah and justice is more acceptable to the Lord than sacrifice* (Prov. 21:3). It is not written 'as much as sacrifice' but *more than sacrifice* (*ibid.*). How? Sacrifices were done only when the Temple was standing but *Tzedakah* and justice were done while the Temple was standing and when it was not. Another explanation: sacrifices are only for sins which were committed by mistake but *Tzedakah* and justice atone for sins committed by mistake and on purpose. Another explanation: sacrifices are practiced only by the lower ones [human beings] but *Tzedakah* and justice by the higher ones [angels] and the lower ones. Another explanation: sacrifices are done only in this world but *Tzedakah* and justice are done in this world and the world to come."[10]

From the above texts we can observe that *Tzedakah* had a special status among the *mitzvot* and was highly valued. Nevertheless, in comparing *Tzedakah* to the other *mitzvot* it should be noted that the Rabbis considered *Gemilut Ḥasadim* to be an even greater *mitzvah*.

---

[9] *Ibid.*

[10] *Devarim Rabbah* 5:3.

CHAPTER FOURTEEN: *TZEDAKAH* IN RESPECT TO SHABBAT AND FAST DAYS

Shabbat was the most joyous and festive day of the week. The Rabbis urged their fellow Jews to save their most elaborate meals for *Shabbat.* Thus a Jew was encouraged to set aside the most delicious foods available and the best wine for this sacred day. However, the poor may not be able to afford any of these items. If the best meal should be on *Shabbat,* what should a poor person do? The question is raised of whether the poor individual should fast on *ᶜErev Shabbat* in order to have enough food for the special meals of *Shabbat.*

> "R. Ḥidka [said], We say to him, What you wish to eat on *ᶜErev Shabbat*, eat on *Shabbat.* And the whole day of *ᶜErev Shabbat* we make him fast? Rather, do as suggested by R. ᶜAkiva who said, Make your *Shabbat* a weekday and do not be in need of other creatures."[1]

During the rabbinic era an individual was expected to eat fifteen meals a week, two meals a day on six days of the week and three meals on *Shabbat.* However, if a poor person had sufficient food for two meals for a day, s/he must not accept food from the *tamḥui* and if he has sufficient food for fourteen meals s/he must not accept money from the *kupah.*[2] Consequently, what happens when a poor person at the beginning of the sixth day of the week (Thursday evening) has only enough food for four meals? Should he eat one of the meals on Thursday evening and fast all of Friday morning and Friday afternoon in order to have three meals on *Shabbat*? Given the above situation, R. ᶜAkiva believed that an individual

[1] *Babylonian Talmud*, Shabbat 118a.

[2] *Ibid.*

should not fast on Friday, but should have two meals on the sixth day and two meals on *Shabbat.*

It was the position of R. ʿAkiva that *Shabbat* should be like a weekday by having the regular two meals rather than having three meals on *Shabbat* if the alternative was to either fast on Friday or obtain additional food through *Tzedakah.* R. ʿAkiva expressed the view that one should avoid dependence on others if at all possible. One should of course endeavor to make *Shabbat* a special occasion with festive meals. However, if this can only be attained by receiving *Tzedakah* one should refrain from such dependence upon others. The better course of action is to keep one's *Shabbat* meals simple and similar to weekday meals. The extra foods and festive meals are not absolutely required on *Shabbat* and may be deleted if they can only be obtained through *Tzedakah.*

On Friday afternoon the family was usually extremely busy with their preparations for *Shabbat.* Nevertheless, even at this time it was permissible for the alms collectors to pay a visit to the home, "As was said by R. Naḥman in the name of Rabbah b. Avuha, because the alms collectors can take a pledge for a *Tzedakah* contribution even on *ʿErev Shabbat.*"[3]

Tzedakah is such an important *mitzvah* that certain aspects of it can even be performed on *Shabbat* itself. "Surely R. Ḥisda and R. Hamnuna both said, In regard to accounts of a religious matter, one is allowed to calculate them on *Shabbat*; and R. Eleʿazar said: One may assign *Tzedakah* to the poor on *Shabbat.*"[4]

The justification for dealing with these financial considerations on *Shabbat* was that these were "accounts" of religious matters concerning the entire community and not the personal affairs of any individual. This type of activity was not deemed to be a desecration of *Shabbat.* From the text itself one cannot be certain as to whether the Rabbis only permitted decisions to be made as to the amounts of *Tzedakah* to be assigned to those in need in the community or whether they permitted the actual money of *Tzedakah* to be distributed as well on *Shabbat.*

---

[3] *Babylonian Talmud*, Bava Batra 8b; see also *Babylonian Talmud*, Kiddushin 76b.

[4] *Babylonian Talmud*, Ketubbot 5a.

In any event, it is interesting to note that even on *Shabbat* one could discuss certain financial transactions and make certain financial decisions. *Tzedakah* is one of the few activities sanctioned in this realm.

> "Is speech forbidden? R. Ḥisda and R. Hamnuna both said: Accounts in connection with a *mitzvah* may be calculated on *Shabbat*. And R. Eleʿazar said, One may assign *Tzedakah* to the poor on *Shabbat*. And R. Yaʾakov b. Idid said in R. Yoḥanan's name: One may supervise matters of life and death and matters of communal urgency on *Shabbat*. Also R. Shmuʾel b. Naḥmani said in R. Yoḥanan's name … One may make arrangements on *Shabbat* for the betrothal of young girls and the elementary education of a child and to teach him a trade! Scripture says, *not pursuing your* [*own*] *business, not speaking thereof* (Isa. 58:13); your affairs are forbidden, the affairs of Heaven are permitted."[5]

In Isa. 58:13 one is urged to make *Shabbat* a delight and not to engage in one's personal business or even to speak about the matter. However, the Rabbis interpreted *Tzedakah* and the other activities listed as not falling into that category but rather as doing work on behalf of God. The Rabbis were well aware that the dire poverty of the poor interfered with the joyous quality of *Shabbat*. On occasion, *Shabbat* could be an especially bad day for the poor.

> "R. Yehoshuʿa b. Levi asked, *All the days of the poor are evil* (Prov. 15:15)? — Surely there are *Shabbatot* and Festivals. However, the biblical verse is true according to Shmuʾel, for R. Shmuʾel said, A change of diet is the beginning of sickness."[6]

Sabbaths and festivals would not necessarily contradict the verse in question that *All days of the poor are evil* (Prov. 15:15). During the week the poor would subsist on meager rations, perhaps only dry bread. If they ate meat or other expensive foods on *Shabbat* they could become extremely ill.

Tragically the poor were in such dire circumstances that they were grateful for virtually any improvement in their condition.

---

[5] *Babylonian Talmud*, Shabbat 150a

[6] *Babylonian Talmud*, Bava Batra 146a.

"And R. Yitzḥak said, Sunshine on the *Shabbat* is *Tzedakah* for the poor, as it is said, *But unto you that fear My name shall the sun of Tzedakah arise with healing in its wings* (Mal. 3:20)."[7] For the poor just having a warm, sunny day, especially on *Shabbat*, was considered to be *Tzedakah* from God. There was an interrelationship between fast days and the giving of *Tzedakah*. It was customary on fast days to give *Tzedakah* equivalent to the value of the food saved during the fast. Thus "Mar Zutra says, The merit of a fast day lies in the *Tzedakah* dispensed."[8]

Furthermore, on fast days, as on all other days, the Rabbis were concerned with promptly dispersing *Tzedakah* to the hungry poor. This was especially true in regard to food that could quickly spoil. This attitude is reflected in the commentary to the following verse, *She was full of justice, Tzedek lodged in her, but now murderers* (Isa. 1:21). "If on a fast day, the distribution of *Tzedakah* is postponed overnight, it is just as though blood was shed, for it is written, *She that was full of justice, Tzedek* (*ibid.*). This applies only to bread and dates, but in the same case of money, wheat or barley it does not matter."[9]

The Hebrew word for lodge, *yalin*, in the above verse has the meaning of staying overnight. The Rabbis made a wordplay on the verse and stated that if one kept the *Tzedakah* proceeds overnight — i.e., postponed overnight — it was equivalent to murder since the desperate poor may starve to death during the delay. The Rabbis were concerned about the urgency of distributing *Tzedakah* (see chapter six). This sense of urgency, however, applied only to food that would readily spoil. Finally, fasting and *Tzedakah* are compared in the following text: "R. Ele῾azar also said, Fasting is greater than *Tzedakah*. What is the reason? One is performed with a person's money, the other with his/her body."[10] Like *Gemilut Ḥasadim* fasting requires more physical effort than the act of giving *Tzedakah*.

---

[7] *Babylonian Talmud*, Ta῾anit 8b.

[8] *Babylonian Talmud*, Berakhot 6b.

[9] *Babylonian Talmud*, Sanhedrin 35a.

[10] *Babylonian Talmud*, Berakhot 32b.

CHAPTER FIFTEEN: BIBLICAL FIGURES PERFORMING *TZEDAKAH*

Since *Tzedakah* was so highly valued within the rabbinic world the Rabbis turned to the Bible to find role models. Hebrew Scripture was their most sacred and holy text and the biblical figures within it could be a source of inspiration to the Rabbis' fellow Jews. Various biblical stories served as vehicles of instruction; through their actions some of the biblical figures demonstrated the nature and value of *Tzedakah*. For example, one of the reasons that Noah was called *Tzadik*, righteous (Gen. 6:9), was that he gave food to God's creatures during the time of the flood. His feeding of the animals on the ark during the deluge has been characterized as an act of *Tzedakah*.[1]

Although the first biblical patriarch, Abraham, had some critical flaws, he was frequently utilized by the Rabbis as an example of an exceptionally good human being. This was illustrated in their stories of how Abraham practiced *Tzedakah*. In the following text Abraham is compared to David in this regard.

> "Moreover, Abraham our father would first practice *Tzedakah* and then justice, as it is said, *For I have known him to the end that he may command his children and his household after him that they may keep the way of the Lord, to do Tzedakah and justice* (Gen. 18:19). When two litigants would come before Abraham our father for judgment and one would say of his fellow, He owes me a *minah*, Abraham our father would take out a *minah* of his own, give it to him, and say to them, Arrange your claims before me. Then each would arrange his claims. In the event that the de-

[1] *Tanḥuma*, ed. Buber, Noaḥ 31, *Tanḥuma*, Noaḥ 5.

> fendant was found owing the other a *minah*, Abraham would say to the one with the *minah*, Give the *minah* to your fellow. But if it was not so, he would say to them, Divide the sum between you and depart in peace.
>
> King David on the other hand did not act in this manner. Instead he would first practice justice and then *Tzedakah*, as it is said, *And David executed justice and Tzedakah unto all his people* (2 Sam. 8:15). When litigants came for judgment before King David, he would say to them, Arrange your claim. In the event that one was found owing his fellow a *minah* [David] would give him a *minah* of his own. And if not, he would say to them, Divide the sum between you and depart in peace."[2]

In the above passage the Rabbis contrasted two biblical verses to demonstrate a point about the character of Abraham and David. In the verse referring to Abraham (Gen. 18:19), *Tzedakah* is mentioned prior to justice. In the verse concerning David (2 Sam. 8:15), the word order is reversed and justice precedes *Tzedakah*. Since nothing is accidental in the Bible, the Rabbis noticed the reversal in word order in regard to these two verses and utilized a story to explain the difference. They concluded that the text indicated that Abraham's first priority was *Tzedakah* while David's was justice.

The above text describes a tension between *Tzedakah* and justice. The Rabbis believed that these values were not necessarily compatible in every respect. They needed to be reconciled and David's life was an example of such reconciliation. David's technique was "arbitration." In this context "arbitration" precludes a strict or harsh implementation of the law. David's objective was to attain a result in which the interests of both parties were taken into consideration and that "arbitration" would lead to peace between the parties.

> "What is that kind of justice that contains peace? One must say that it is arbitration. So it was with David, as Scripture says, *And David executed justice and Tzedakah unto all his people* (2 Sam. 8:15). Surely where there is [strict] justice there is no *Tzedakah*,

[2] *Avot de Rabbi Natan* 33, version a, Schechter edition.

> and where there is *Tzedakah*, there is no justice. What is the kind of justice which contains *Tzedakah*? One must say, arbitration.
>
> However, the following explanation of this verse will accord with the first *Tanna* [who holds arbitration to be prohibited]. In judging, [David] used to acquit the guiltless and condemn the guilty; but when he saw that the condemned man was penniless, he helped him out of his own funds. This is *justice and Tzedakah* (*ibid.*) — justice to one by awarding him his money and *Tzedakah* to the other by paying out of his own funds. And therefore Scripture says about David, *David practiced justice and Tzedakah unto all his people* (*ibid.*) … Indeed, even if he had not paid for him out of his own funds, he would nevertheless have executed justice and *Tzedakah*; justice to the one by awarding him his money and *Tzedakah* to the other by freeing him from a robbed thing in his possession."[3]

The above passage shows a unique twist to the idea of *Tzedakah*. If the person who was liable to the other party could not pay, David would give him money in order to pay his just debt. If the person who was liable to the other party had money, David would compel him to practice *Tzedakah*. The *Tzedakah* would free him from his ill-gotten gains. The "*Tzedakah*" would be given to the party from whom he had wrongfully taken the money.

Yose b. Yoḥanan of Jerusalem said, "Let your house be opened wide and let the poor be members of your household."[4] The first portion of this text is examined in context of the story of Job.

> "Let your house be opened wide? How? This teaches that a person's house should have a wide entrance on the north, south, east, and west, like Job's, who made four doors to his house. And why did Job make four doors to his house? So that the poor would not be troubled to go all around the house, one coming from the north could enter on his way, one com-

---

[3] *Babylonian Talmud*, Sanhedrin 6b.

[4] *Mishnah*, Avot 1:5.

> ing from the south could enter on his way, and so in all directions. For that reason Job made four doors to his house."[5]

The easy access of Job's home enabled the poor to readily obtain *Tzedakah*. Although Job gave *Tzedakah*, he was not as magnanimous as Abraham in this regard. Abraham exceeded the expectations of the donee, while Job supplied the donee with the minimum required under the circumstances. This was brought to Job's attention at the time that he protested to God that he was not deserving of his series of misfortunes.

> "Now when that great calamity came upon Job, he said unto the Holy One, blessed be He, Master of the Universe, did I not feed the hungry and give the thirsty to drink; as it is said, *Or have I eaten my morsel myself alone and the fatherless has not eaten thereof?* (Job 31:17) And did I not clothe the naked, as it is said, *As if he were not warmed with the fleece of my sheep?* (Job 31:20)
>
> Nevertheless the Holy One, blessed be He, said to Job, Job you have not reached half of the measure of Abraham. You sit and remain in your house and the wayfarers come in to you. To him who is accustomed to eat wheat bread, you give wheat bread to eat; to him who is accustomed to drink wine, you give wine to drink. But Abraham did not act this way. Instead he would go forth and make the rounds everywhere, and when he found wayfarers he brought them into his house. To him who was unaccustomed to eat wheat bread, he gave wheat bread to eat; to him who was unaccustomed to drink wine, he gave wine to drink. Moreover he arose and built big palaces on the roads and left there food and drink, and every passerby ate and drank and blessed Heaven. That is why delight of spirit was given to him. And whatever one might ask for was to be found in Abraham's house, as it is said, *And Abraham planted a tamarisk tree in Beer-Sheba* (Gen. 21:33)."[6]

---

[5] *Avot de Rabbi Natan*, 7, version a, Schechter edition.

[6] *Ibid.*

In addition to giving more than what was expected Abraham did not passively wait for the poor to approach his home. Unlike Job who merely waited for the poor to arrive at his home, Abraham actively sought out the poor in order to bring them into his home.

When biblical figures did practice *Tzedakah* they were often handsomely rewarded by God. Isaac is utilized by the Rabbis to demonstrate the rewards of *Tzedakah*.

> "*And Isaac sowed in that land* (Gen. 26:12). Rabbi Eliᶜezer said, Did Isaac sow the seed of grain? Heaven forbid! But he took all his wealth and sowed it in *Tzedakah* to the poor, as it is said, *Sow yourselves according to Tzedakah, reap according to Ḥesed* (Hos. 10:12). Everything which is tithed, the Holy One, blessed be He, returned him one hundred times in money and blessed him, as it is said, *And he found in the same year hundredfold; and the Lord blessed him* (Gen. 26:12)."[7]

[7] *Pirke de Rabbi Eliᶜezer*, 33.

CHAPTER SIXTEEN: RESTRICTIONS UPON THE DONEE AND RECEIVING *TZEDAKAH* FRAUDULENTLY

In chapter eight it was explained that there are certain restrictions, expectations and obligations placed upon the donor in regard to *Tzedakah*. Since the donors did not have infinite resources and the needs of the poor were not completely satisfied by existing systems of *Tzedakah*, the Rabbis were compelled to place certain restrictions, expectations and obligations upon the donee as well.[1]

Not every person could accept *Tzedakah*. One had to fall below a certain "poverty line" to be eligible. If an individual had enough food to eat, even for the short term, s/he could not take food or money. These resources had to be limited to those in desperate need. "If a person has food enough for two meals s/he may not take anything from the *tamḥui*, and if enough for fourteen meals he may not take from the *kupah*."[2]

In addition to her/his actual food supply the Rabbis took into consideration her/his total financial circumstances. If a person had a minimum net worth, s/he was ineligible to accept certain types of *Tzedakah*. "If a person had two hundred *zuz* s/he may not take gleanings, the forgotten sheaf, *pe'ah* or the poorman's tithe; if s/he has two hundred less one *denari* and even a thousand [donors] together gave her/him each [one *denar*], he may take [gleanings, the forgotten sheaf, *pe'ah* or the poorman's tithe]."[3]

---

[1] See also Aharon Lichtenstein, "The responsibilities of the recipient of charity," *ʿAlei Etzion* 16 (2009) 7–30.

[2] *Mishnah*, Pe'ah 8:7.

[3] *Ibid.*, 8:8.

However, there were three exceptions to the above rule that a net worth of at least two hundred *zuz* disqualified a potential donee from receiving from the gleanings, the forgotten sheaf, *pe'ah* or the poorman's tithe. First, "if his goods were pledged to his creditor or were security for his wife's *Ketubah*, he may take [gleanings, the forgotten sheaf, *pe'ah* or the poorman's tithe]."[4] Under these circumstances, the donee's assets are frozen; s/he has no liquid assets to purchase the necessities of life.

Second, "if a person had 50 *zuz* and s/he traded with them, s/he may not take [gleanings, the forgotten sheaf, *pe'ah* or the poorman's tithe]."[5] In this case, an individual could be disqualified if s/he had as little as 50 *zuz* if s/he used them in commercial trade. We can speculate that since s/he was already negotiating in business, s/he could probably barter for her/his necessities during commercial transactions. In the alternative, s/he may not be able to continue her/his business without a monetary reserve.

Third, regardless of the actual wealth of the individual, s/he may be in transit and temporarily without any cash.

> "If a householder was traveling from one place to another and it became necessary for her/him to take gleanings, the forgotten sheaf, *pe'ah* or the poorman's tithe, s/he may take them, and when s/he returns to her/his house s/he should make restitution. So [states] R. Eliᶜezer, but the Sages say, [He need make no restitution because] at that time s/he was a poor person."[6]

The last sentence raises the issue of whether an individual may retain certain assets and still receive *Tzedakah*. Must an individual surrender virtually all of her/his property before s/he can properly take *Tzedakah*? The rabbinic response: "They may not compel a person to sell her/his house or his articles of service."[7] Thus, the recipient could retain her/his house and household furnishings and still be able to accept *Tzedakah*. Nevertheless, the exemption of a

---

[4] *Ibid.*, 8:8.

[5] *Ibid.*, 8:9.

[6] *Ibid.*, 5:4.

[7] *Ibid.*, 8:8.

home and its furnishings could be the subject of abuse. In the *Talmud* is found the following rabbinic remedy to this potential problem.

> "We learnt elsewhere: They may not compel her/him to sell her/his house or her/his articles of service. May s/he not? Was it not taught: If s/he was in the habit of using gold utensils s/he shall now use silver ones, if [s/he was using] silver ones let her/him now use copper ones?"[8]

This approach combines a sensitivity to the prior economic circumstances of the donee (see chapter eight) with the realistic appraisal that some adjustment is inevitable when one becomes poor.

Previously in this chapter it was pointed out that generally there was a "poverty line" of two hundred *zuz*. A mischievous or malicious person could take advantage of this rule and circumvent the spirit of *Tzedakah*. This is illustrated in the following text which gives examples of improper behavior.

> "What is a foolish pietist like? — For example, when a woman is drowning in the river, and he says, It is improper for me to look upon her and rescue her. What is a cunning rogue like? — R. Yoḥanan says, He who explains his case to the judge before the other party to the suit arrives. R. Abahu says, S/he who gives a poor person a *denar* to bring his/her possession to two hundred *zuz*, for we have learnt: S/he who possesses two hundred *zuz* may not take gleanings, forgotten sheaves, *pe'ah* or the poor person's tithe; but should s/he lack one *denar* of the two hundred, even if a thousand persons give him/her [the gleanings, etc.] simultaneously, s/he may take it."[9]

Thus by giving him just one *denar*, the donee becomes ineligible to receive a thousand *denari* if there were that many potential donors who were willing simultaneously to each give her/him one *denar*. Another restriction upon a donee is if s/he receives the *Tzedakah* under certain conditions from the donor. If the *Tzedakah* is given

---

[8] *Babylonian Talmud*, Ketubbot 68a.

[9] *Babylonian Talmud*, Sotah 21b.

for a specific purpose then the donee is obligated to comply with that purpose.

> "But it is this [dictum] of R. Meir, for it has been taught: R. Shimᶜon b. Eleᶜazar said to R. Meir's authority: If one gives a *denar* to a poor person to buy a shirt, s/he may not buy a cloak with it, to buy a cloak, s/he must not buy a shirt, because s/he disregards the opinion of the owner [donor]. But perhaps there it is different, because s/he may fall under suspicion. For people may say, So-and-so promised to buy a shirt for that poor person, and has not bought it, or So-and-so promised to buy a cloak for that poor person, and has not bought it. If so, it should state, Because s/he may be suspected. Why state, Because s/he disregards the owner's [donor's] desire? This proves that it is because s/he makes a change, and s/he who disregards the owner's [donor's] desire is called a robber."[10]

The question raised in the above rabbinic debate is whether the donor retains any ownership rights in the *Tzedakah* after s/he has given it to the donee. If the *Tzedakah* is totally unconditional, the donee should be able to use the money or any other item received according to his wishes. One school of thought is that the donor's gift is conditional and that if the donee does not use the *Tzedakah* according to the expressed intentions of the donor s/he is actually stealing from the donor. The counter argument to this is that the donor does not really have any ownership interests in the *Tzedakah*; it was given unconditionally. However, the donee should act responsibly and not embarrass the donor. If the donor has made a promise or commitment to help an individual in a certain manner and that promise or commitment becomes known to a third party, then the donee should not take actions that would contradict the position of the donor. It should be noted that this situation would even arise if the donor gave *Tzedakah* in secret or anonymously (see chapter seven).

An implicit expectation of every donor of *Tzedakah* is that the donee actually is in need of assistance. As stated above, it is prohibited to take *Tzedakah* if one has certain economic assets, but sup-

---

10 *Babylonian Talmud*, Bava Metziah 78b.

pose one does anyway. The Rabbis believed in divine retribution for such an act.

> "S/he that does not need to take them yet takes them shall not depart from this world before s/he falls in need of her/his fellow human being; but s/he that needs to take them yet does not take them shall not die in old age before s/he has come to support others out of her/his own goods. Of such a one it is written, *Blessed be the person that trusts in the Lord, and whose hope the Lord is* (Jer. 17:7). And if a person is not lame or blind or halting, yet makes himself/herself like to one of them, as it is written, *But he that searches after mischief it shall come unto him* (Prov. 11:27). And again it is written, *Justice, justice shall you follow* (Deut. 16:20)."[11]

The above sense of "poetic justice" is echoed in the thoughts of Rabbi ʿAkiva. "R. ʿAkiva says, Whoever takes a *perutah* from *Tzedakah* when s/he does not need it, shall depart from this world before s/he falls in need of her/his fellow creatures. "He used to say, He that binds rags on his eyes or his loins and cries, Give to the blind, to the afflicted, shall in the end be speaking the truth."[12]

The Rabbis were reluctant to be victimized in their efforts to disperse *Tzedakah*. For example, "R. Abba used to bind some *zuz* in his scarf, put it on his back and place himself at the disposal of the poor. He cast his eye sideways because of rogues."[13] One ingenious viewpoint about rogues is reflected in the following story:

> "R. Ḥanina had a poor person to whom he regularly sent four *zuz* on *ʿErev Shabbat*. One day he sent that sum through his wife who came back and said to him that there was no need for it. What did you see? [She replied], I heard that he was asked, On what will you dine, on the silver linen or on the gold one? R. Ḥanina said, This is why R. Eleʿazar said, Come let us be grateful to the rogues for were it not for them we would

---

[11] *Mishnah*, Peʾah 8:9.

[12] *Avot de Rabbi Natan* 3, version a, Schechter edition.

[13] *Babylonian Talmud*, Ketubbot 67b.

> have been sinning every day, for it is said, *And he cry unto the Lord against you, and it be sin to you* (Deut. 15:9)."[14]

This biblical verse indicates that it is a sin not to give *Tzedakah*. However, it is not a sin if in fact the "donee" is attempting to obtain *Tzedakah* fraudulently. Under these circumstances the Rabbis taught that the defrauding donee will actually create a self-fulfilling prophecy. By claiming to be physically afflicted he will ultimately bring upon himself this very same affliction. "Our Rabbis taught: If a person pretends to have a blind eye, a swollen belly or a bent leg, s/he will not depart from this world before actually coming into such a condition. If a person accepts *Tzedakah* and is not in need of it, s/he shall in the end not depart from this world before s/he comes to such a condition."[15]

---

[14] *Ibid.*, 67b–68a.

[15] *Ibid.*, 68a.

CHAPTER SEVENTEEN: *TZEDAKAH* AND THE GENTILE COMMUNITY

As can be seen from the discussion in chapter twelve, there was a Talmudic dispute as to whether *Tzedakah* by Gentiles should be viewed in good light. One point of view was that Gentiles may have evil motives such as to dominate or shame Israel. In this perspective, *Tzedakah* by Gentiles is perceived as a negative phenomenon, even a sin. Rabbi Yoḥanan b. Zakai ultimately held that *Tzedakah* when practiced by Gentiles atones for their sins. The tension in regard to these two different viewpoints is found in other rabbinic passages. For example, "When those who accepted *Tzedakah* from Gentiles multiplied, Israel moved to the top and they below, Israel went forward, and they backward."[1] This passage may be understood on at least two levels. On a literal level there is a sense of gloating that perhaps Israel is exploiting those same people who are attempting to dominate it. On another level this could be a sarcastic remark in which the author regrets the humiliation of Israel accepting *Tzedakah* from Gentiles and being dependent upon them.[2] The sentence then should be understood in exactly the opposite manner from what it actually says. The anger at the Gentiles is evinced in this passage:

> "Rava gave the following explanation, What is the meaning, *But let them be overthrown before You; deal thus with them in the time of Your anger* (Jer. 18:23) — Jeremiah spoke before the Holy One,

---

[1] *Babylonian Talmud*, Sotah 47b.

[2] Elliot N. Dorff, "A Jewish theology of Jewish relations to other peoples." In: *Peoples of God: A Jewish-Christian Conversation in Asia* (ed. Hans Ucko; Geneva: WCC Publications, 1996), 46–66.

> blessed be He, Master of the Universe, even when they do *Tzedakah*, cause them to be frustrated by people unworthy of any consideration so that no reward be forthcoming to them for that *Tzedakah*."[3]

One reason for the anger against Gentiles was their ridicule of what the Rabbis deemed to be sacred. "All that ridicules the Torah and the holy and the feasts and nullifies the covenant with Abraham, our father, will not have a part of the World to Come, even if s/he has done good works."[4]

In addition, Gentiles and Jews during the rabbinic era did not have the same perspective towards *Tzedakah*. Christianity did not use *Tzedakah* as a mechanism to create fundamental social change. For example, James 2:15–16 states: "If you know someone who needs clothes or food, you should not say: 'I hope all goes well for you. I hope you will be warm and have plenty to eat.' What good is it to say this, unless you do something to help?" Poverty was not considered as an evil which should be eradicated. Poverty, in some respects, was even praiseworthy in its ascetic quality. As discussed earlier, the rabbinic view of poverty was that it degraded humanity and *Tzedakah* was a method of repairing the world. The Rabbis accepted that there would be both rich and poor within their society but they felt that the tensions between the various classes could be reduced by means of *Tzedakah*. *Tzedakah* could be utilized to reduce social inequalities and to strengthen the sense of mutual responsibility and community among Jews.[5]

Furthermore, not all the references in respect to *Tzedakah* and Gentiles are negative. For example, there is the story of Ifra Hormiz, a Gentile, who offered *Tzedakah* to the Jewish community. After some debate by the Rabbis her *Tzedakah* was accepted.

> "R. Ya^cakov b. Aḥa said in R. Asi's name: It is forbidden to help [Gentiles] or act as their agents. Rava said, We may teach them: Ifra Hormiz, the mother of King Shapur, sent an offer-

---

[3] *Babylonian Talmud*, Bava Kama 16b.

[4] *Avot de Rabbi Natan* 35, version b, Schechter edition.

[5] E. E. Urbach, "Political and Social Tendencies in Talmudic Concepts of Charity," *Zion* 16 (1951), 1–27 (Hebrew).

> ing to Rava saying that it should be offered in honor of Heaven. Rava said to R. Safran and R. Aḥa b. Huna: Go, bring two young [Gentile] men … and offer [their offering] up in honor of Heaven."[6]

Additionally, for the sake of peace between the two communities, *Tzedakah* was shared between the Jews and the Gentiles. According to *Tosefta*, *Gittin* 3:13–14, it is recommended that Gentiles should be provided with *Tzedakah*, including the burial of their dead.[7] The *Talmud* elaborates: "The poor of the Gentiles are not prevented from gathering gleanings, forgotten sheaves and the *pe'ah* to avoid ill feeling. Our Rabbis taught: We support the poor of the Gentiles and the poor of Israel, and visit the sick of the Gentiles and the sick of Israel and bury the poor of the Gentiles and the poor of Israel, in the interests of peace."[8]

This interdependence between the Jewish and Gentile communities is also illustrated by the following text. "It was taught: In a city with Jewish and Gentile inhabitants one appoints Gentile and Israelite alms collectors and they collect from Gentiles and from Israelites. And they support the Gentile poor and the Israelite poor and bury the Gentile and the Israelite dead and comfort the Gentile and the Israelite mourners."[9]

---

[6] *Babylonian Talmud*, Zevaḥim 116b.

[7] *Tosefta*, Pe'ah 3:1, ʿEruvin 5:11, Nedarim 2:7, ʿAvodah Zarah 1:3, Ḥullin 10:13.

[8] *Babylonian Talmud*, Gittin 61a.

[9] *Talmud Yerushalmi*, Gittin 5:9, 33a.

CONCLUSION

According to the Jewish tradition as expressed in classical rabbinic literature, belief in God shatters egocentricity. The self-centered individual is precluded from establishing and maintaining a relationship with God. This relationship or covenant with God requires a Jew to be responsive to the needs of others. *Tzedakah* is the instrumentality to educate and sensitize Jews in respect to the needs of others.

Over and over again the rabbinic texts that we have examined emphasize the human dignity of every individual. This is perhaps the key to understanding the rabbinic concept of *Tzedakah*. We all have an obligation to enhance the lives of others so that they may live in dignity. Poverty has the potential of undermining an individual's sense of dignity and self-worth. Since we have received the gift of life from God, as well as many other gifts, we have the responsibility of participating in *Tikun ʿOlam*, the repair of the world. The system of *Tzedakah* as created and implemented by the Rabbis is a paradigm of how we can attack the evil of poverty. Selfishness and its concomitant attitude of indifference to the needs of others has the potential of destroying humanity. *Tzedakah* has the potential of redeeming humanity. Maimonides states:

> "Whoever sees a poor person asking [for assistance] and ignores him and does not give him *Tzedakah* has transgressed a negative commandment as it is written, d*o not harden you heart nor shut your hand against your needy brother* (Deut. 15:7)."[1]

[1] Maimonides, *Mishneh Torah*, Hilkhot matenot ʿaniyim, 7:2.

RABBINIC AUTHORITIES

Antigonos of Sokho, first half of the third century BCE
Abba, c. 290
Abba b. Yirmeah, Babylonia, c. 270
Abaye, Babylonia, c. 338
Abba Shaul, c. 150
Abba Yudan, c. 90
Abun, Israel, c. 325
Ada bar Ahavah, Babylonia, c. 250
Aḥa, Israel, c. 320
Aḥa b. Huna, Babylonia, c. 300/400
Aivo, Israel, c. 320
ᶜAkiva, Israel, c. 135
Ammi, Israel c. 300
Ashi, Babylonia, c. 427
Asi, Baylonia, c. 250
Avuha, Babylonia, c. 250
Bar Kappara, Israel, c. 220
Bar Merion, c. 300
Berekhia, Israel, c. 340
Bibi, Israel, c. 320
Dimi, Israel, c. 320
Elᵓai, Israel, c. 110
Eleᶜazar, several Rabbis are named E., e.g., Israel, c. 270
Eleᶜazar b. R. Shimᶜon, Israel, c. 180
Eleᶜazar Ha-Kappar, Israel, c. 180
Eliᶜezer, several Rabbis are named E., e.g., Israel, c. 90
Eliᶜezer b. Birtah, Israel, c. 110
Eliᶜezer b. Yaᶜakov, Israel, c. 150
Gamliel b. Rabbi, Israel, c. 220
Ḥama b. R. Ḥanina, Israel, c. 260
Hamnuna, Babylonia, c. 300

Ḥanina, Israel, c. 380
Ḥanina b. Teradion, Israel, c. 135
Ḥidka, Israel, c. 120
Hillel the Elder, Israel, c. 20 BCE
Ḥisda, Babylonia, c. 309
Ḥiyya, Israel, c. 280
Hoshaʿyah, Israel, c. 300
Huna, several Rabbis are named H., e.g., Babylonia, c. 297
Isi, several Rabbis are named I., e.g., Israel, c. 150
Kahana, several Rabbis are named K., c. 250
Leʿazar b. R. Yose, c. 180
Levi, Israel, c. 300
Lulianus of Dromeah [Julianus from the south?], Israel, c. 320
Mar ʿUkba, Babylonia, c. 270
Mar Zutra, Babylonia, c. 320–419
Mar Zutra b. Tuviah, c. 270
Meir, Israel, c. 150
Naḥman, c. 400
Naḥman b. Yitzḥak, Babylonia, c. 356
Naḥum of Gamzu, Israel, c. 90
Natan b. Abba, Babylonia, c. 270
Natan b. Ammi, Babylonia, c. fourth century
Pinḥas b. Ḥama, Israel, c. 360
Rabbah b. Avuha, Babylon c. 280
Rabbah Tosfaʾah, Babylonia, c. 468–470
Rav, Babylonia, c. 247
Rava, Babylonia, c. 352
Ravina, Babylonia, several Rabbis are named R., e.g., c. 420
Safran, Israel, c. third century
Shila, Babylonia, c. 210
Shiloh of Noveh, c. fourth century
Shimʾon b. Ḥalafta, Israel, c. 190
Shimʿon, c. 280
Shimʿon b. Eleʿazar, Israel, c. 190
Shimʿon b. Gamliel, Israel, c. 140
Shimʿon b. Lakish, Israel, c. 250
Shmuʾel, see Shmuʾel bar Naḥmani
Shmuʾel b. Naḥman, Israel, c. 260
Shmuʾel b. Yehudah, Babylonia, c. 280
Shmuʾel bar Naḥmani, Israel, c. 260

Tanḥum b. R. Ḥiya, Israel, c. 300
Tanḥuma, Israel, c. 380
Tarfon, Israel, c. 110
Ya'akov b. Aḥa, c. fourth century
Ya'akov b. Idid, Israel, c. 280
Yannai, Israel, c. 225
Yehoshuʿa, c. 90
Yehoshuʿa of Sikhnin, Israel, c. 330
Yehuda Ha-Nasi (Judah the Prince), Israel, c. 135–219.
Yirmeah b. Eleʿazar, Israel, c. 270
Yishmaʾel, c. 135
Yitzḥak, Israel, c. 300
Yoḥanan, Israel, c. 279
Yoḥanan bar Nappaḥa, Israel, third century
Yoḥanan ben Zakai, Israel, c. 80
Yonah, Israel, c. 350
Yose b. Kismal
Yose b. Yoḥanan of Jerusalem, c. 150 BCE
Yose ben Ḥalafta, Israel, c. 150
Yosef, c. 300
Yudah, several Rabbis are named Y., e.g., c. 300
Yudah b. R. Shalom, Israel, c. 370
Yudah bar Simon, Israel, c. 329
Yudan, several Rabbis are named Y., e. g. c. 300

GLOSSARY

ʿam ha-aretz [an ignorant, illiterate person]
Beit Din [rabbinic court comprised of three judges]
Beit Ha-Midrash [house of study]
bikur ḥolim [visiting the sick]
Bozrah [was the capital of Edom]
brit milah [circumcision]
cherub [an angel; the name of a winged being mentioned frequently in the Bible]
denari [denarius; Roman silver coin]
ʿErev [eve of a holy day]
Evil Inclination [the inclination to do evil by violating the will of God]
First tithe [a positive commandment in the Torah requiring the giving of one tenth of agricultural produce, after the giving of the standard *terumah,* to the Kohen or Levite]
Forgotten sheaves [see Deut. 24:19: *When you reap your harvest in your field, and have forgotten a sheaf in the field, you shall not go again to get it: it shall be for the stranger, for the fatherless, and for the widow: that the Lord your God may bless you in all the work of your hands.*]
Gehinom [the name given to Hell in the rabbinic literature. The name was borrowed from that of a valley in Jerusalem]
Gemara [c. 500 CE), an interpretation of the *Mishnah* and related Tannaitic writings]
Gemilut Ḥasadim [acts of loving-kindness]
Gleanings [The custom of allowing the poor to follow the reapers in the field and glean the fallen spears of grain is strikingly illustrated in the story of Ruth (Ruth 2:2–23). This custom derived from one of the early agricultural laws of the Hebrews (Lev. 19:9; 23:22; Deut. 24:19–21)]
Good Inclination [the inclination to follow the will of God]
ḥallah [the priest's share of dough]

Ḥasid [a pious person]
ḥayot ["living beings" mentioned in the prophet Ezekiel's vision of the Chariot]
Ḥesed [loving-kindness]
Hoshaʾna [the seventh day of Sukkot]
Ifra Hormiz [Ifra, possibly from Afghanistan, married Hormazd II, Sassanid Emperor of Persia (302–309 CE)]
ʿisa [a certain amount of flour]
kavanah [motivation]
Ketubah [marriage contract]
King Monobaz [son of Helena of Adiabene, he began to rule in 55 CE).
King Shapur [Shapur I the Great, the second Sassanid King of the Persian Empire, c. 240–272 CE]
kupah [the charity chest]
lulav [is a closed frond of the date palm tree; one of the "Four Species" used during Sukkot. The other species are the myrtle, willow, and *etrog* (citron). When bound together, they are referred to as "the lulav."]
Maḥuza [ancient city formed by Seleucia and Ctesiphon on opposite sides of the Tigris River]
marit ʿayin [appearance to others]
matrona [Roman lady]
Mezuzah [is a piece of parchment inscribed with specified verses from the Torah (Deut. 6:4–9 and 11:13–21), which comprise the prayer "Shemaʿ Yisraʾel", beginning with *Hear, O Israel, the Lord our God, the Lord is One.* A mezuzah is placed in a small container that is affixed to the doorframe of a house)
Nakdimon ben Gorion [Nicodemus ben Gorion, first century CE; the wealthiest and most respected member of the peace party during the revolution in the reign of Vespasian]
Nazirite [refers to a person who voluntarily took a vow described in Num: 6:1–21.]
Peʾah [corner of a field, for the poor]
perutah [a small coin]
Pesaḥ [Passover celebrates the deliverance of the Jewish people from slavery in Egypt]
poorman's tithe [The tithe for the poor gave rise to the tithing of one's earnings]
pulsing [small coins]

Purim [commemorates a time when the Jewish people living in Persia were saved from destruction]
Rosh Ha-Shanah [beginning of the year on the first day of *Tishrei*, the first month of the Jewish calendar. The day is believed to be the anniversary of the creation of Adam and Eve, the first man and woman, and their first actions toward the realization of mankind's role in God's world. Rosh Hashanah customs include sounding the *shofar* and eating symbolic foods]
Second Tithe [In the days of the Temple in Jerusalem, the second tithe involved the setting aside of one tenth of specific agricultural produce from the first, second, fourth, and fifth, years of each seven-year cycle, for the purpose of taking it to the holy city of Jerusalem, and consuming it there]
selaᶜ [a coin]
Seraphim [a category of (flaming) angels]
Shabbat Sabbath, the seventh day of the week [a day of rest]
Shavuᶜot [Feast of Weeks; it commemorates the day God gave the Torah to the entire nation of Israel assembled at Mount Sinai]
Shekhinah [Divine Presence]
Shmoneh Esreh [the "Eighteen Benedictions," a prayer]
shofar [a ram's horn used as a musical instrument]
siyan [gold *denari*]
Sukkah [a temporary hut constructed for use during the week-long festival of *Sukkot*]
Taharah [the ritual washing of the corpse]
Talmid Ḥakham [student]
tamḥui [consisted of the weekly collections for the poor not in money but in kind]
Tanna [a rabbinic sage recorded in the *Mishnah*]
Temple [the First or Second Temple in Jerusalem]
Tikun ᶜOlam [humans should contribute to the "repair of the world"]
Torah [Torah has a range of meanings: it can most specifically mean the first five books of the Hebrew Bible, it can mean this, plus the rabbinic commentaries on it, it can mean the continued narrative from Genesis to the end of the Hebrew Bible, it can even mean the totality of Jewish teaching and practice.]
Tzadik [righteous person]
Turnus Rufus [a Roman governor posted in Judea during the first half of the second century CE]

Usha [In the middle of the second century CE an important synod of rabbinical authorities was convened in the Galilean city of Usha, near Shefarʾam, Tiberias, and Sepphoris]

Yom Kippur ["Day of Atonement," is the holiest day of the year; its central themes are atonement and repentance, fasting and prayer]

Zuzin [ancient Jewish silver coins struck during the Bar Kochba revolt. They were overstruck on Roman Imperial *denarii* or Roman provincial drachmas of Vespasian, Titus, Domitian, Trajan and Hadrian. Four *zuz*, *denarii* or drachmas make a *Shekel*, a *Selaʿ* or a *Tetradrachm*]

BIBLIOGRAPHY

RABBINIC LITERATURE

Avot de Rabbi Natan bi-shte Nusḥaot (ed. Shneur Zalman Schechter), New York, 1967, 2nd ed.; *The Fathers According to Rabbi Nathan* (trans. Judah Goldin; Yale Judaica Series; New Haven: Yale University Press, 1990). *Avot de Rabbi Natan* exists in two recensions ("a" and "b"); it contains ethical material and may be dated to the third century CE.

Babylonian Talmud: Talmud Bavli (Vilna: Romm, 1893); *Babylonian Talmud, 16 vols.* (trans. and ed. I. Epstein; London: Soncino, 1978; repr. of 1935–52 ed.); Avraham Y Katsh, גנזי תלמוד בבלי (Jerusalem: Rubin Mass, 1975). The *Talmud* has two components: the *Mishnah* (c. 200 CE), the first written compendium of Judaism's Oral Law, and the *Gemara* (c. 500 CE), an interpretation of the *Mishnah* and related Tannaitic writings, but the *Talmud* includes aggadic and other material, too. There are numerous commentaries on the Talmudic text. It mainly contains discourses from the Babylonian sages, and it represents the cultural memory of rabbinic Judaism. The *Talmud* consists of 63 tractates.

Bemidbar Rabbah (*Numbers Rabbah*) in *Midrash Rabbah. Numbers Rabbah* is a Midrashic work on the biblical Book of Numbers that consists of two separate parts: sections 1–14 and 15 until the end; the first part is related to the *Tanḥuma* and was redacted around the twelfth century, while the second part dates from the sixth to eighth century.

Bereshit Rabbah (*Genesis Rabbah*)*: Midrash Bereshit Rabba mit Kritischem Apparat und Kommentar* (ed. Theodor, Y. and Albeck, H.; 2nd ed. Jerusalem, 1962; based upon the Frankfurt am Main edition of 1932); *Genesis Rabbah: The Judaic Commentary to the Book of Genesis; A New American Translation, vols. 1–3* (trans. J. Neusner; Atlanta: Scholars Press, 1985). *Genesis Rabbah* was probably redacted in the first half of the fifth century CE; it is an exegetical *Midrash* on parts of the biblical Book of Genesis.

Derekh Eretz Zuta, a non-canonical tractate of the *Babylonian Talmud*; it contains ethical teachings.

Derekh Eretz Rabbah, a non-canonical part of the *Babylonian Talmud*; it contains Tannaitic teachings that are not included in the *Mishnah* or *Tosefta.*

Devarim Rabbah (*Deuteronomy Rabbah*): *Midrash Devarim Rabbah Ed. from the Oxford Ms. No. 147* (ed. Saul Lieberman; Jerusalem, 1974); *Devarim Rabbah* in *Midrash Rabbah. Deuteronomy Rabbah* is a homiletic Midrashic work on the biblical Book of Deuteronomy. It was redacted between 450 and 800 CE.

Eikha Rabbah (*Lamentations Rabbah*) in *Midrash Rabbah*; *Midrasch Echa Rabbati* (ed. S. Buber; Vilna, 1899; repr. Hildesheim: Olms, 1967). *Lamentations Rabbah* is an exegetical *Midrash* on the Book of Lamentations; dated to the fourth/fifth centuries CE.

Kallah Rabbati, one of the minor tractates appended to the end of the fourth order, *Nezikin*, in the printed texts of the *Babylonian Talmud.*

Maimonides, *Mishneh Torah* (Haifa: Mifʿal Mishneh Torah, 2009), Hilkhot matenot ʿaniyim. The *Mishneh Torah*, subtitled *Sefer Yad ha-Ḥazaka*, is a code of Jewish law (*halakhah*) by Maimonides (referred to as *RaMBaM*, an acronym for Rabbi Moshe ben Maimon). The *Mishneh Torah* was compiled between 1170 and 1180, while Maimonides was living in Fustat, Egypt. The work consists of fourteen books, subdivided into sections, chapters and paragraphs. It is the only medieval work that details all of Jewish observance, including those laws which are only applicable when the Temple is in place.

Mekhilta: Mekilta de Rabbi Ishmael: A Critical Edition on the Basis of the MSS and Early Editions … with an English Translation, Introduction and Notes (ed. and trans. Jacob Z. Lauterbach; Philadelphia: The Jewish Publication Society, 1933–35; repr. 2004); *Mekhilta de-Rabbi Yishmaʾel* (ed. Ḥayyim Shaul Horovitz and Yisrael Avraham Rabin; 2nd ed., Jerusalem, 1970).

Midrash Rabbah (Vilna: Romm, 1887; reprint Jerusalem, 1961); *Midrash Rabbah* vols. 1–10 (eds. of the translation, H. Freedman and Maurice Simon, London: Soncino Press, 1939). *Midrash Rabbah* is a collection of Midrashic works on the Pentateuch and on the five scrolls (*Song of Songs*, *Ruth*, *Lamentations*, *Ecclesiastes*, *Esther*).

Midrash Shoḥer Tov ʿal Mishle (ed. S. Buber; Vilna 1890; repr. Jerusalem, 1967). *Midrash Proverbs* or *Aggadat Mishle* is an exegetical *Midrash* on the biblical Book of Proverbs; it is dated to the eighth century.

Midrash Shoḥer Tov ʿal Tehillim (ed. S. Buber; Vilna 1890; repr. Jerusalem, 1967); *The Midrash on Psalms*, vols. 1–2 (trans. William G. Braude; New Haven: Yale University Press, 1959). *Midrash Tehillim*, called also *Aggadat Tehillim*, as well as *Shoḥer Tov* because of its opening verse, Prov. 11:27, is an aggadic Midrashic work on the Psalms. Dated to the seventh century and later, although its concluding section is from the thirteenth century.

Midrash Tanḥuma (printed edition). *Midrash Tanḥuma* (ed. Hanokh Zundel; repr. Jerusalem, 1974); A. Kensky, *Tanhuma ha-nidpas* (Ph. D. Diss., The Jewish Theological Seminary, New York, 1990). *Tanḥuma* is a homiletic Midrashic collection interpreting the weekly readings from the Pentateuch; it is dated between the sixth and seventh centuries and later. Presently, there exist two major versions: the so-called "printed edition" and the material included in the Buber edition (see below).

Midrash Tanḥuma. Midrash Tanhuma Ha-Kadum Ve-Ha-Yashan (ed. S. Buber, Vilna, 1885; repr. Jerusalem, 1964); *Midrash Tanhuma*, 3 vols. (trans. John Townsend; Hoboken, NJ: Ktav, 1989–1997). *Tanḥuma* is a homiletic Midrashic collection interpreting the weekly readings from the Pentateuch; it is dated between the sixth and seventh centuries and later.

Midrash Zutah ʿal Shir ha-Shirim, Rut, Ekhah ve-Qohelet … ʿim nusḥa sheniyah ʿal megilat Ekhah … va-ʿalehem nilvah Yalquṭ Shimʿoni ʿal Ekhah (ed. S. Buber; Berlin: Mekitze Nirdamim, 1895). *Song of Songs Zuta* is an aggadic Midrashic work on passages from the biblical Book of *Song of Songs* and it is dated to the end of the tenth century or earlier.

Mishnah: Ḥanokh Albeck, ed., *Shishah Sidre Mishnah* vols. 1–6 (Jerusalem, 1959; rpt., 6 Jerusalem, 1988); *The Mishnah* (trans. Herbert Danby London: Oxford University Press, 1933); Jacob Neusner, *The Mishnah: A New Translation*. (New Haven: Yale University Press, reprint 1991). The *Mishnah* is dated to c. 200 CE; it is a systematic compilation of Jewish law (*halakhah*).

Pesikta de Rav Kahana: *Pesiqta de-rav kahana*, 2 vols. (ed. Dov Mandelbaum, New York: The Jewish Theological Seminary, 1962); *Pesikta de-Rab Kahana: R. Kahana's compilation of discourses for Sabbaths and festal days* (trans. William G. Braude and Israel J. Kapstein; Philadelphia: Jewish Publication Society). *Pesikta de Rav Kahana* is a homiletic Midrashic works based upon the festivals and the special Sabbaths of the liturgical calendar; the core of the work is dated to the fifth century CE and parts of it may be dated to the twelfth/thirteenth centuries.

Pesikta Rabbati: *A Synoptic Edition of Pesiqta Rabbati Based Upon the Extant Manuscripts and the Editio Princeps*, 3 vols. (ed. Rivka Ulmer, Atlanta: Scholars Press, and Lanham: University Press of America, 1998–2000; repr. Lanham: University Press of America, 2008); *Pesikta Rabbati, discourses for feasts, fasts, and special Sabbaths*, 2 vols. (trans. William Braude; New Haven: Yale University Press, 1968). *Pesikta Rabbati* is a homiletic Midrashic works based upon the festivals and the special Sabbaths of the liturgical calendar; the core of the work is dated to the fifth century CE and parts of it may be dated to the twelfth/thirteenth centuries.

Pirke de Rabbi Eliezer: *The Chapters of Rabbi Eliezer the Great* (trans. Gerald Friedlander; New York: Sepher-Hermon Press, 1981, 4th ed.; 1st ed., London, 1916); *Mishnat Rabbi Eliᶜezer* (New York: Bloch, 1969). *Pirke de Rabbi Eliezer* is a Midrashic work that was redacted under Islamic influence in the eighth /ninth centuries; it contains exegetical passages and retellings of the Pentateuch.

Qohelet Rabbah (*Ecclesiastes Rabbah*) in *Midrash Rabbah*. *Ecclesiastes Rabbah* is an exegetical *Midrash* on verses from the biblical Book of Ecclesiastes; it was probably redacted not earlier than the eighth century CE.

Ruth Rabbah in *Midrash Rabbah*. *Ruth Rabbah* is dated to the sixth century or earlier; it is a homiletic and aggadic interpretation of verses from the biblical Book of Ruth.

Seder Eliyahu rabah ve-seder Eliyahu zuṭa ha-muva ʾim be-shem Tana de-ve Eliyahu (ed. Meir Friedmann; Vienna: self-published, 1902–04).

Seder Olam Rabbah (ed. B. Ratner; Vilna, 1897; repr. Jerusalem, 1988). *Seder Olam Rabbah* is a c. second century CE chronology detailing the dates of biblical events from the Creation to the conquest of Persia by Alexander the Great.

Shemot Rabbah (*Exodus Rabbah*) in *Midrash Rabbah*; *Midrash Shemot rabbah, chs. 1–14* (ed. A. Shinan; Tel-Aviv, 1984). *Shemot Rabbah* is a Midrashic work that was redacted in the tenth century. It consists of two different compositions: sections 1–14 are rewritten parts of the so-called *Tanḥuma-Yelammedenu* literature in the style of exegetical *Midrash*; sections 15 until the end also belong to this literature.

Shir Rabbah (*Canticles Rabbah*) in *Midrash Rabbah*; *Midrash Shir ha-Shirim* (ed. E. Halevi Grünhut; Jerusalem, 1981). *Shir Rabbah* is also known as *Midrash Ḥazita*; it is an aggadic Midrashic compilation on the biblical Book *Song of Songs* dated between 300–1100.

Shulḥan Arukh, compendium of Jewish law by Joseph Karo (1488 Toledo, Spain — 1575 Safed, Land of Israel).

Sifré Deuteronomy: L. Finkelstein, ed., *Siphre ad Deuteronomium* (Berlin, 1939; repr. New York, 1969); Reuven Hammer, trans., *Sifre: A Tannaitic Commentary on the Book of Deuteronomy* (New Haven: Yale University Press, 1986). Sifré to Deuteronomy is a verse by verse exegetical *Midrash* to the Book of Deuteronomy, a probable date for the work is *c.* 300 CE.

Sifré Numbers: H. S. Horovitz (ed.), *Sifre de-Ve Rav, I. Sifre ʿal Sefer Bemidbar Ve-Sifre Zutah* (Leipzig, 1917; repr. Jerusalem, 1966). Sifré to Numbers is a verse by verse exegetical *Midrash* to the Book of Numbers.

Tosefta: M. S. Zuckermandel, ed., *Tosefta ʿal pi Kitve Yad Erfurt U-vin* (Pasewalk, 1880; repr. with suppl. by S. Lieberman, Jerusalem: Sifrei Wahrman, 1970); Saul Lieberman, *The Tosefta according to Codex Vienna*, 4 vols. (New York: The Jewish Theological Seminary, 1955–73); Saul Lieberman, *Tosefta Kifeshuṭa*: *A Comprehensive Commentary on the Tosefta,* Vol. 5 (New York: The Jewish Theological Seminary, 1962). A Tannaitic work that consists of a compendium of Jewish law, similar to the *Mishnah.* The *Tosefta* was compiled around 220 CE. It corresponds to the *Mishnah* in its divisions of *sedarim* ("orders") and *masekhot* ("tractates").

Vayikra Rabbah (*Leviticus Rabbah*) in *Midrash Rabbah*; *Midrash Vayyiqra Rabbah* (ed. M. Margulies (Margaliot); New York and Jerusalem: Jewish Theological Seminary of America, 3rd printing,

1993). Redacted between 400 and 500 CE, *Leviticus Rabbah* is a homiletic Midrashic work to passages from the biblical Book of Leviticus.

Yerushalmi: *Talmud Yerushalmi* (Krotoszyn: Monasch, 1866). *The Talmud of the Land of Israel: A Preliminary Translation and Explanation* (ed. Jacob Neusner; Chicago Studies in the History of Judaism; Chicago: University of Chicago Press, 1982–1991); Peter Schäfer, et al., *Synopse zum Talmud Yerushalmi*, vols. 1– (Tübingen: Mohr/Siebeck, 1991–). The *Yerushalmi* (also known as the *Palestinian Talmud* or *Jerusalem Talmud*) was redacted no later than 370 CE. This *Talmud* contains an analytical commentary on the Mishnah. The *Yerushalmi*, the *Talmud* of the Land of Israel was developed over the course of nearly 200 years by the Talmudic Academies in the Land of Israel (principally those of Tiberias and Caesarea). The sages of these Academies devoted considerable attention to analysis of the agricultural laws of the Land of Israel.

SECONDARY LITERATURE

Alexander, Philip, "Quid Athenis et Hierosolymis? Rabbinic *Midrash* and Hermeneutics in the Greco-Roman World." In: *A Tribute to Geza Vermes* (eds. P. R. White and R. T. Davies; Sheffield: Sheffield Academic Press, 1990), 101–24.

Alon, Gedaliah, *The Jews in their Land in the Talmudic Age* (Cambridge, Mass.: Harvard University Press, 1989).

Anderson, Gary, A., *Charity: The Place of the Poor in the Biblical Tradition* (New Haven: Yale University Press, 2013).

Baskin, Judith, *Midrashic Women: Formation of the Feminine in Rabbinic Literature* (Hanover, NH: University Press of New England, 2002).

Becknell, Robert B., *Almsgiving, the Jewish Legacy of Justice and Mercy* (PhD diss. Miami University-Ohio, 2000).

Ben-Shalom, Menachem, "Matan tzedakah shel ḥasidim le'or Avot de-Rabbi Natan version alef." In: Yuval Shaḥar, ed., בארץ ובתפוצות בימי בית שני ובתקופת המשנה; ספר זיכרון לאריה כשר (Tel-Aviv, 2012), 275–94. (Hebrew)

Bokser, Baruch M., *Post Mishnaic Judaism in Transition: Samuel on Berakhot and the Beginnings of the Gemara* (Atlanta: Scholars Press, 1980).

Bowker, John, *The Targums and Rabbinic Literature: An Introduction to Jewish Interpretations of Scripture* (Cambridge: Cambridge University Press, 2009).

Boyarin, Daniel, *Intertextuality and the Reading of Midrash* (Bloomington: Indiana University Press, 1990).

Brooks, Roger, *Support for the Poor in the Mishnaic Law of Agriculture: Tractate Peah* (Chico, CA: Scholars Press, 1983).

Cohen, Shaye, *From the Maccabees to the Mishnah* (Louisville, KY: Westminster John Knox, 2006).

Cronbach, Abraham, "Judaism and Social Justice Historically Considered," *Central Conference of American Rabbis Yearbook*, vol. 25 (1915), 3–11.

Cronbach, Abraham, "The Gradations of Benevolence," *Hebrew Union College Annual* 16 (1941), 163–86.

Cronbach, Abraham, "The Meʾil Zedakah (Second Article)," *Hebrew Union College Annual* 12–12 (1938–1939), 635–96.

Cronbach, Abraham, *Religion and its Social Setting* (Cincinnati: The Social Press, 1933).

Daube, David, "Alexandrian Methods of Interpretation and the Rabbis." In: *Essays in Greco-Roman and Related Talmudic Literature* (ed. H. A. Fischel; New York: Ktav, 1977), 23–44.

Dorff, Elliot N., "A Jewish theology of Jewish relations to other peoples." In: *Peoples of God: A Jewish-Christian Conversation in Asia* (ed. Hans Ucko; Geneva: WCC Publications, 1996), 46–66.

Elbaum, Jacob, "From Sermon to Story; the Transformation of the Akedah," *Prooftexts* 6 (1986), 97–116.

Encyclopedia Judaica, 16 vols. (Jerusalem: Keter, 1971–1972; revised edition: Gale, 2007).

Feinstein, Joseph, *Am I My Brother's Keeper?* (New York: Jewish Education Committee Press, 1970).

Fishbane, Michael, *The Garments of Torah: Essays in Biblical Hermeneutics* (Bloomington: Indiana University Press, 1989).

Frisch, Ephraim, *An Historical Survey of Jewish Philanthropy, From the Earliest Times to the Nineteenth Century* (New York: The MacMillan Company, 1924).

Gardner, Gregg Elliot, *Giving to the Poor in Early Rabbinic Judaism* (PhD diss. Princeton, 2009).

Gereboff, Joel, *Rabbi Tarfon, the tradition, the man, and early Rabbinic Judaism* (Missoula, MT: Scholars Press, 1979).

Ginzberg, Louis, *Legends of the Jews*, 7 vols. (trans. Henrietta Szold and Paul Radin; Philadelphia: Jewish Publication Society, 2003, 2nd ed., 1st ed. 1967–1969, repr. of 1909 edition).

Goldberg, Arnold, "Form-analysis of Midrash Literature as a Method of Description," *Journal of Jewish Studies* 36 (1985), 159–74.

Gray, Alyssa M., "Redemptive Almsgiving and the Rabbis of Late Antiquity," *Jewish Studies Quarterly* 18 (2011), 144–84.

Halivni, David Weiss, "Sof hora'ah — the end of teaching what?" *Educational Deliberations: Studies in Education Dedicated to Shlomo (Seymour) Fox* (eds. M. Nisan and O. Schremer; Jerusalem: Keter, 2005), 76–83.

Hartman, Geoffrey and Sanford Budick (eds.), *Midrash and Literature*, New Haven: Yale University Press, 1986).

Harris, Jay, "From Inner-Biblical Interpretation to Early Rabbinic Exegesis." In: *Hebrew Bible, Old Testament: The History of Its Interpretation* (ed. Magne Sæbo; Göttingen, 1996), Vol. 1, 256–69.

Hezser, Catherine, *The Social Structure of the Rabbinic Movement in Roman Palestine* (Tübingen: Mohr/Siebeck, 1997).

Hirshman, Marc, "On the Nature of Mitzva and its Reward in the Mishnah and Tosefta" (Hebrew), *Proceedings of the Tenth World Congress of Jewish Studies, Division C*, vol. 1 (Jerusalem, 1990), 54–60.

Hoffman, David, *Mishnah Rishonah: Die erste Mischna und die Controversen der Tannaim, von D. Hoffmann; aus Anlass seines 70-jährigen Geburtstages namens seiner Schüler ins Hebräische übers., von Samuel Grünberg* (Jerusalem, 1967). (Hebrew)

Holtz, Barry W., *Back to the Sources: Reading the Classic Jewish Texts* (Philadelphia: The Jewish Publication Society, 1984).

Jacobs, Irving, *The Midrashic Process: Tradition and Interpretation in Rabbinic Judaism* (New York: Cambridge University Press, 1995).

The Jewish Encyclopedia (New York: Funk and Wagnalls, 1901–1905). http://www.jewishencyclopedia.com/

Kalmin, Richard, "The post-Rav Ashi Amoraim: transition or continuity? A study of the role of the final generations of Amoraim in the redaction of the Talmud," *AJS Review* 11 (1986), 157–87.

Kaplan, Mordecai M., "Jewish Philanthropy: Traditional and Modern." In: Farris, E., Laune, F., and Todd, A. (eds.), *Intelligent Philanthropy* (Chicago: University of Chicago Press, 1930).

Kindler, Arieh, "A Bar Kokhba Coin Used as a Charity Token," *Israel Numismatic Journal* 12 (1992–93), 73–75.

Kraemer, David C., "The Mishnah." In: *The Cambridge History of Judaism* IV (2006) 299–315.

Kugel, James, "Two Introductions to *Midrash*," *Prooftexts* 3 (1983), 131–55.

Levine, Lee I., *The Rabbinic Class of Roman Palestine in Late Antiquity* (Jerusalem: Yad Itzḥak Ben-Tzvi Publications, 1989).

Lichtenstein, Aharon, "The responsibilities of the recipient of charity." In: *ʿAlei Etzion* 16 (2009), 7–30.

Margaliot, Reuben, *Yesod ha-Mishnah va-ʿarikhatah: seḳirah kelalit ʿal hishtalshelutah mi-yemot anshe keneset ha-gedolah ʿad ḥatimatah, ve-tokhnit sidurah* (Jerusalem: Mosad ha-Rav Kook, 1955). (Hebrew)

Massyngberde, Ford J., "Three ancient Jewish views of poverty." In: *New Way of Jesus* (Newton, Kan: Faith and Life Press, 1980), 39–55.

Nelson, David W. and Rivka Ulmer (eds.), *Re-presenting Texts: Jewish and Black Biblical Interpretation: Proceedings of the 2010 and 2011 SBL Midrash Sections* (Piscataway, NJ: Gorgias Press, 2013).

Neusner, Jacob (ed.), *The Babylonian Talmud: A Translation and Commentary*, 22 Vols. (Peabody, MA: Hendrickson Publishers, 2005).

Neusner, Jacob (ed.), *The Talmud of the Land of Israel: A Preliminary Translation and Explanation* (Chicago Studies in the History of Judaism; Chicago: University of Chicago Press, 1982–1991).

Neusner, Jacob, *From Literature to Theology in Formative Judaism: Three Preliminary Studies*, (Atlanta: Scholars Press, 1989).

Neusner, Jacob, "The formation of rabbinic Judaism: from the Mishnah's philosophy to the Talmud's religion." In: *Or le-meʾir* (Shamir Yona; Beer Sheva: Ben Gurion University of the Negev Press, 2010), 121–41.

Neusner, Jacob, *Introduction to Rabbinic Literature* (New York: Doubleday, 1994).

Neusner, Jacob, *Invitation to Midrash: The Workings of Rabbinic Bible Interpretation* (Atlanta: Scholars Press, 1992).

Neusner, Jacob, *Judaism: The Evidence of the Mishnah* (Chicago: University of Chicago Press, 1981).

Neusner, Jacob, *Making the Classics in Judaism* (Atlanta: Scholars Press, 1989).

Neusner, Jacob, *Torah: From Scroll to Symbol* (Atlanta: Scholars Press, 1988).

Novick, Michael, "Charity and reciprocity: structures of benevolence in rabbinic literature." *Harvard Theological Review* 105 (2012), 33–52.

Porton, Gary G., "Definitions of *Midrash*." In: *Encyclopedia of Midrash*, Leiden: Brill, 2005), vol. 1, 520–34.

Porton, Gary, *The Traditions of Rabbi Ishmael* (Leiden: E. J. Brill, 1982).

Raphael, Marc Lee (ed.), *Agendas for the Study of Midrash in the Twenty-First Century* (Williamsburg, Va.: College of William and Mary, 1999).

Rosenthal, Franz, "Sedaka, Charity," *Hebrew Union College Annual* 23 (1950/51), 411–30.

Safrai, Shmuel; Safrai, Zeev; Schwartz, Joshua; and Tomson, Peter J., *The Literature of the Sages. Part One: Oral Torah, Halakha, Mishna, Tosefta, Talmud, External Tractates* (Compendia Rerum Iudaicarum Ad Novum Testamentum; Minneapolis: Fortress, 1987; 2007. *Second Part.* Assen: Van Gorcum, 2006).

Satlow, Michael L., "'Fruit and the fruit of fruit': charity and piety among Jews in Late Antique Palestine," *Jewish Quarterly Review* 100, 2 (2010), 244–77.

Schäfer, Peter, *The History of the Jews in the Greco-Roman World* (London: Routledge, 2003).

Peter Schäfer, et al. (eds.), *Synopse zum Talmud Yerushalmi*, vols. 1– (Tübingen: Mohr/Siebeck, 1991–).

Schechter, Solomon, *Aspects of Rabbinic Theology … introduction by Neil Gillman* (Woodstock, Vt.: Jewish Lights, 1999; repr. of the first edition, Philadelphia: The Jewish Publication Society, 1909).

Schochet, Jacob I., *Gemilut Chassadim* (Brooklyn, NY: Kehot Publications, 1967)

Schwartz, Seth, *Imperialism and Jewish Society 200 BCE to 640 CE* (Princeton, NJ: Princeton University Press, 2001).

Seccombe, David, "Was there Organized Charity in Jerusalem before the Christians?" *Journal of Theological Studies* 29 (1978), 140–43.

Segal, Eliezer Lorne, "Rabbi Eleazar's 'perutah'," *Journal of Religion* 85 (2005), 25–42.

Shinan, Avigdor, "The Tale of the Citrons," *Meḥkere Yerushalayim be-folklor yehudi* 13/14 (1990/91), 61–79. (Hebrew)

Sperber, Daniel, *Roman Palestine: 200–400. The Land* (Ramat-Gan: Bar Ilan University Press, 1978).

Stemberger, Günter, *Introduction to the Talmud and Midrash* (Edinburgh: T& T Clark, 1996, 2nd edition).

Stern, David, *Midrash and Theory. Ancient Jewish Exegesis and Contemporary Literary Studies* (Evanston: Northwestern University Press, 1996).

The Dynamics of Tzedakah (Jerusalem: The Shalom Hartmann Institute for Advanced Judaic Studies, 1981).

Ulmer, Moshe, *The Rabbinic Concept of Tsedakah* (Rabbinical Thesis; Hebrew Union College — Jewish Institute of Religion, Cincinnati, 1988).

Ulmer, Rivka, "Charity." In: *Reader's Guide to Judaism.* (Chicago: Fitzroy Dearborn, 2000), 108–10.

Ulmer, Rivka, "Discourse in *Midrash*: Textual Strategy and the Use of Personal Pronouns in Halakhic *Midrash*," *Approaches to Ancient Judaism, N.S.* 13 (1998), 51–70.

Ulmer, Rivka, "*Pesiqta Rabbati*: A Text Linguistic and Form-Analytical Analysis of the Rabbinic Homily," *Journal of Jewish Studies* 64 (2013), 64–97.

Ulmer, Rivka, "The advancement of arguments in exegetical *Midrash* compared to that of the Greek ΔΙΑΤΡΙΒΗ [diatribe]," *Journal for the Study of Judaism* 28,1 (1997), 48–91.

Ulmer, Rivka, "Theological Foundations of Rabbinic Hermeneutics." In: *Encyclopedia of Midrash*, vol. 2, 944–64.

Ulmer, Rivka, *Egyptian Cultural Icons in Midrash* (Studia Judaica, Forschungen zur Wissenschaft des Judentums 52; Berlin & New York: Walter de Gruyter, 2009).

Urbach, Ephraim E., "Political and Social Tendencies in Talmudic Concepts of Charity." (Hebrew), *Zion* 16 (1951), 1–27

Urbach, Ephraim E., *The Sages: Their Concepts and Beliefs* (Cambridge: Harvard University Press, 1987).

Visotzky, Burton L., *Golden Bells and Pomegranates* (Tübingen: Mohr/Siebeck, 2003)

Weinfeld, Moshe, *Social Justice in Ancient Israel and in the Ancient Near East* (Jerusalem, 1995), 33–39.

Zunz, Leopold, *Die gottesdienstlichen Vorträge der Juden historisch entwickelt … 1892* (repr. Piscataway, NJ: Gorgias, 2003), xxi–xxxviii.